Let Me Ask You This...

Let Me Ask You This

Conversations
That Draw
Couples Closer

Chap & Dee Clark

NAVPRESS ●
A MINISTRY OF THE NAVIGATORS
P.O.BOX 35001, COLORADO SPRINGS, CO 80935

The Navigators is an international Christian organization. Jesus Christ gave His followers the Great Commission to go and make disciples (Matthew 28:19). The aim of The Navigators is to help fulfill that commission by multiplying laborers for Christ in every nation.

NavPress is the publishing ministry of The Navigators. NavPress publications are tools to help Christians grow. Although publications alone cannot make disciples or change lives, they can help believers learn biblical discipleship, and apply what they learn to their lives and ministries.

Cover photograph: Comstock, Inc.

All Scripture in this publication is from the *Holy Bible: New International Version* (NIV). Copyright © 1973, 1978, 1984, International Bible Society. Used by permission of Zondervan Bible Publishers.

Printed in the United States of America

CONTENTS

PREFACE

Like many other couples, when we first got married, we made several commitments to each other. Among them was the commitment to make the friendship in our marriage the highest earthly priority in our lives. We were determined not to let our careers, children, friends, or interests rob us of the reason we came together in the first place. We set a course to maintain this commitment at all costs.

This decision went hand in hand with our mutual faith in Jesus Christ. We were aware of the biblical admonitions regarding the supremacy of Christ even above our spouses, but we felt that many couples had taken that counsel too far. Yes, our personal faith in Christ is number one in priority, but we believe that it must be lived out in the way we love each other.

As we have walked together for several years and through many experiences — three children, two moves, major job changes, developmental choices — we have been able to maintain at least this one promise to each other. We are closer than we have ever been. We are more in love with each other than when we began this journey. With all the disappointments and failures, life has been a thrilling adventure because we are together. We are best friends, we are colaborers, we are partners, and we love Jesus together.

There is no real secret. We haven't stumbled on the hot, new trick of keeping marriages intact. Two main things have kept us together: We dialogue as often as possible about everything, and we allow our faith in Christ to dwell at the center of our relationship.

This book, then, is our gift to those who could use a catalyst, a spark, to rebuild and reclaim their friendship. Our prayers are with you as you seek to love each other.

ACKNOWLEDGMENTS

This book was not our idea; it was the brainchild of two of our closest friends. They felt that we had two things to share with the world: a deep and powerful friendship at the core of our marriage, and Dee's uncanny ability to ask probing questions. As the four of us dreamed of how to get other couples talking, especially about their faith within the context of marriage, the conviction for this book began to grow.

David and Josi Larson, we are forever indebted to you for pushing us into this project and ministry to marriages.

We also want to thank those couples who helped us think through the format, gave helpful criticism of the content, and prayed with and for us. We believe this has been a team project from day one, and we are very grateful.

As we consider the source of any insight or ministry we may have, it is primarily the Lord we have to thank. Scripture has been our foundation since the day we met. But God has also used many others to teach us of His desire for marriage. So to all who have taught us and touched us by your example, we thank you.

HOW TO USE THIS BOOK

This book is a tool. It is not an attempt to tell you how or what to think about a given issue. Each chapter is short, only two or three pages, and the structure is very simple. The intent is to provide you as a couple with a resource, so you can come to Scripture together and discuss how it impacts your lives—both corporately and as individuals. Don't let a comment or statement slow you down, but let these words stimulate you to express your own opinions, hopes, and dreams as you interact with your spouse, and as you pray together.

We've left to your discretion how often you would like to use this book. Some couples may spend almost every evening going through a topic as a way to end their day, and others may spend only one evening a week. We would like to encourage you, however, to take a few moments together at least twice a week. We are convinced that the more often you use this little book, the deeper your friendship will become.

We strongly encourage you to read the next section, "How to Talk to Your Spouse," before you begin looking at the topics. This section provides groundrules for a helpful, healthy discussion and will enhance the time you have together.

TITLE, SCRIPTURE, AND DEVOTIONAL

The first page of each session provides a framework for the topic. There is a subject title and a brief passage of Scripture, which you may want to refer to if you desire a sense of context, but it is not essential to do so. The remainder of the page is a brief devotional commentary on both the Scripture passage and the topic.

We suggest that you read this section together, either out loud or sitting side by side. We believe it is important for you to use this devotional as a springboard for your discussion, so it is best to read it together as you go.

CONVERSATION STARTER

The "Conversation Starter" is nothing more than a possible response any husband or wife could have to the topic. Again, we suggest that you read them together to keep you "on the same page." While this section does contain a specific viewpoint, we do not wish to put words in your mouth, nor do we want to start a debate between you and this mythical opinion.

Our hope is that this section will provide you with something to spur your thoughts and feelings and to help crystalize what you think. You may totally disagree with what is expressed, and that is fine, so long as it is an encouragement for you to discover and express to your spouse what *you* think and feel.

LET ME ASK YOU THIS . . .

Now it is *your* turn! This is where you have the opportunity to talk with one another. We have given you a few questions to get you started, and to keep you going if you get stuck. But, again, *this book is simply a tool!* So, once you are talking and sharing what it is you are thinking and feeling, you have accomplished the main purpose of the book. If a question doesn't fit your situation, go on to another one, or make up one yourself.

A Suggested Prayer

To ensure that a couple is not only growing in their friendship but also in their mutual devotion and commitment to Christ, we believe that prayer is essential, so we have included a suggested prayer. Not everyone will need or want someone else to tell them how to pray, and that is fine. But because some individuals may be relatively new to conversational, verbal prayer with their spouse, we have offered this section as a possible alternative. You can use it to begin praying along the direction of the topic.

One Last Thought

There is no set way to use this book. You could take it on a weekly date with each other, read it in bed before you say goodnight, or grab a few minutes after dinner with a cup of coffee. For those who would like to journal their way through these topics, for example, you could get two notebooks and write down your answers before talking about them. You are the ones who will make this book fit your situation.

There is not even a "right" order of topics. If you want to skip around and choose your own, that's great. You may find it helpful, once you have completed the book, to go back in a year or two and redo each issue. You may be surprised how your perspective will have changed.

But don't let this be one more book that sits on the shelf. Give it your best shot for the first few times together. Don't be discouraged if sometimes it just doesn't seem to fly. Relationships are difficult and complex, and even the best of intentions are subject to our schedules, moods, and circumstances. Keep trying, keep talking, and keep praying.

HOW TO TALK
TO YOUR SPOUSE

As we have been involved in marriage seminars and conferences, it has struck us how different couples are. Some can talk with ease, some the men dominate, and some the women. And then there are those who cannot seem to communicate at all.

One thing is sure, however: Everybody struggles with communication in marriage. Everybody fights, disagrees, and argues. The trick is learning how to struggle in a way that is loving, gentle, and doesn't attack your spouse. There is always room to grow. Often, the only way we will allow ourselves to grow is through conflict.

God has not left us on our own to pull this off. He has given us a foundation upon which to build every relationship, and it is also the bedrock of any loving discussion:

> If you have any encouragement from being united with Christ, if any comfort from his love, if any fellowship with the Spirit, if any tenderness and compassion, then make my joy complete by being like-minded, having the same love, being one in spirit and purpose. Do nothing out of selfish ambition or vain conceit, but in humility consider others better than yourselves. Each of you should look not

only to your own interests, but also to the interests of others.

Your attitude should be the same as that of Christ Jesus. (Philippians 2:1-5)

With these words in mind, here are eight groundrules for having a discussion with your spouse.

GROUNDRULES FOR COMMUNICATION

Beware Interrupting Each Other

We all have a natural tendency to want to be heard, especially when what we hear sparks a thought. We must do all we can to not only hold back from interrupting until our partner is finished speaking, but to also continue to *listen*. Once we allow our minds to hang on to one word or issue, there is no way that we can lovingly hear what is being said, and we block communication.

Beware the Temptation for One Person to Dominate

By definition a discussion is when two people share thoughts and ideas with one another. The idea of this type of discussion is *not* to win, it is to understand each other and to grow together as friends. The spouse who is more verbal should ensure that there is equal participation in the discussion, but you both must make this a high priority.

Use Word Pictures to Describe Feelings that Are Hard to Communicate

One husband, in trying to let his wife know how difficult it is to start a new business, compared his work to the birth of their child: Just as she was "taken away" from him due to the demands of the baby (nursing, etc.) and for a season he felt separated from her, so, too, his business demanded that type of attention, which she could not share with him. Because he used such a vivid picture, she immediately understood how he felt.

Even the use of a single word to describe a feeling

may be a helpful tool. Words like *dark, alone,* or *impatient* are ways to communicate how you feel. Or utilize a combination of these, "I feel like a new kid in school—there's no one to talk to." The more we use word pictures to tell our story, the better chance we will have at being heard and understood.

When an Issue Begins to Divide You, One Person Must Take on the Role of the Objective Narrator

Our style has been to try to look at issues as being "out there," separate and distinct from our relationship. If we feel as though we are beginning to lose perspective, we will sometimes place an object on the coffee table, sit side by side holding hands, and talk about the issue as symbolized by the object before us. We need to remind ourselves that we are not the enemy, or even adversary; we are two people who love each other trying to come together.

This is usually the crux of marriage communication—someone must be willing to step back and objectively talk about "The Issue," and eventually both must be willing to let go of their position, or there will never be movement. As you begin to feel yourself digging in your heels, ask yourself this question, "Is this a ditch I am willing to die in?" If not, then do whatever it takes to step back and work it through.

Feelings Are Neutral, and Therefore It Does No Good to Try and Argue Them Away

For the most part, we have very little control over our feelings, and it is important to be able to share them with someone we love. People—especially men—sometimes have a tendency to try to explain away feelings, or worse yet, to think we can rebuke them logically. Both partners must have the freedom and be willing to openly talk about the feelings we experience, no matter how hard it may be. You will discover feelings are never quite as potent when they are openly discussed and dealt with.

When Sharing, Do All You Can
Not to Attack Your Spouse

We are responsible for our own feelings. Often we hear, "I told him my feelings: He makes me so mad!" But that is not really true. A woman's husband doesn't make her *anything*; she has responded to her environment by getting angry. In a case like this, if she were to tell her husband, "When you do that, I find myself getting mad!" she has not so much attacked him as she has told him how she feels. As subtle as this distinction is, working hard to avoid statements that attack will make it easier for the other person to bypass defensiveness.

Even when we say the "right" words, we may use a host of other ways to subtly attack our spouse during a discussion. Our body language, eye contact, gestures, and tone of voice all communicate volumes. Is our desire to come together or to attack? Because we can never hide our hearts, it is imperative that we constantly examine our attitudes as we talk.

When You Hit a Crossroads,
Don't Allow a New Thought Until You Have
Adequately Repeated What Has Been Said So Far

Once a discussion moves into phrases such as, "Yes, but . . . ," communication is as good as dead. Instead of defensive or explanatory phrases, try to really hear what the other person is saying. Respond to them with something like, "Are you saying that when I don't phone, you feel that I don't care?" and wait for a response. When you have correctly identified the feeling, then you are ready to move to the next issue—"Thanks for letting me know that. What is going through my head when I don't phone is. . . ."

It Takes Time to Talk

As obvious as it seems, the biggest reason couples have a hard time talking is a lack of adequate time to deal with issues as they arise. It is more expedient to argue and fight than it is to listen carefully and work through misunderstandings. At least weekly, and more often if possible, give yourselves time for constructive discussion—you need time to fight, argue, and disagree. Your disagreements will be less destructive and your good times better, when you care enough to walk together through every issue. *A6*

IN CONCLUSION

If you come to an impasse, or don't seem to be making any progress as you discuss these topics, come back and reread this chapter. Discuss the quote from Philippians 2 and these groundrules. If you still cannot seem to break through to each other, seek out a counselor you both trust, and let that person help you to sort out the issues that keep you from being able to talk.

A friend recently defined marriage as "Two selfs jockeying for turf." Marriage is one of life's greatest laboratories. There are few places where we are forced to deal with our own pride and selfishness. If you entered marriage with the idea that "love will conquer all," you probably didn't really know what that would mean. But it is true; love is the opposite of selfishness, and if we are willing to deny ourselves and seek more to understand than to be understood, our love will win out.

ANXIETY

Do not be anxious about anything, but in everything, by prayer
and petition, with thanksgiving, present your requests to God.
And the peace of God, which transcends all understanding,
will guard your hearts and your minds in Christ Jesus.

Philippians 4:6-7

♡

"If only this one deal goes through, we'll be in great
shape!" I had heard this before. This guy's remark
at a men's prayer breakfast did not reflect a one-
time sentiment, it was his prayer nearly every week! As a
salesman, he constantly lived on the edge, or so it seemed,
waiting for the "big deal" that would push him closer
to . . . closer to . . . nobody quite knew just what.

We don't hear the word *anxious* much anymore, but
we still carry its mark. The most obvious symptom is a
bad case of the "If only's" — "If only we had more money.
If only Bob got that job. If only we had more time. . . ."

Our search for the kind of security that is able to free
us from worry is a never-ending quest for the mythical
pot of gold at the end of the rainbow. Many search and
struggle, trying to capture its reward, only to discover
that the quest is a lie. This cultural pilgrimage is taking
place all around us, and to fight it is to swim upstream.

The issue is not so much our pace as our focus. When
life has been reduced to nothing more than chasing a
dream, we cannot escape the torment of worry. The rainbow of peace can be found, but it can never be manipulated, controlled, or purchased. It is the result of letting
go, coming to the end of our rope and jumping into the

waiting arms of God the Father. Once we throw the weight of our burdens on Him, we receive what we so desperately need—the peace of God.

CONVERSATION STARTER

In the hustle and bustle of everyday life, a man seeking peace and calm may say something like this:

Husband

I worry about a lot of things: how we are doing financially, how I am going to accomplish all the things I need to get done, and how to control my weight—just to list a few. My answer has been to plow ahead and try to solve as much as I can as fast as I can, hoping there will be an end to it. But there rarely is. I need the Lord Jesus to take from me those things that I carry and cannot release.

A woman may have a different reaction to anxiety, as expressed here:

Wife

My answer to anxiety is to compartmentalize things—to place those things that cause me to worry in a nice, rationalized box and push it out of sight so that I don't have to deal with it. But I know that, over time, they will usually resurface, or I will eventually become numb to my feelings.

LET ME ASK YOU THIS ...

- How do you define "anxiety"? "Anxious"? Describe what it feels like when you experience these emotions.
- Are there any specific things in your life right now that are causing you to feel anxious? How can I help you?
- How does your relationship to Jesus Christ impact

those things that worry you? How can we pray together specifically for this?

A SUGGESTED PRAYER

Father God, we confess that we are consumed by many things. We worry about tomorrow, and yet we know that You tell us again and again that You can be trusted. Help us to trust You, and to rely on You for our security . . .

ARGUING

*Joshua said, "Ah, Sovereign LORD, why did you ever bring this
people across the Jordan to deliver us into the hands
of the Amorites to destroy us? If only we had been content
to stay on the other side of the Jordan!"*

Joshua 7:7

O n the face of it, the gall of Joshua, to argue with
the Almighty! To doubt that God knew what He
was doing with the people of Israel, especially for
a leader like Joshua, was a grave statement of unbelief.

But on closer examination, Joshua's outburst was less
a declaration of disillusionment than a plea for understanding. He was not so much arguing with the Lord as
he was confronting the apparent circumstances God had
allowed to take place. In his despair, Joshua sought the
Lord, and his cry arose out of a desire for his Lord to act.
God responded, and Israel defeated her enemies.

Sometimes arguing is healthy. It is rarely fun, and
it can be painful or even destructive, but there is a time
when we need to speak our mind. The attitude, timing,
and manner in which we argue will be the gauge of how
deeply we desire reconciliation and understanding.

Joshua cried out after several hours of prayer and
humble silence. When we are hurt, or feel misunderstood
or mistreated, we, too, may cry out. Like Joshua, we need
to pause, pray, and come to terms with our own baggage
before we "go at it" with the one we love. But, once we
are ready to act with love and tenderness, the best thing
we can do is sit down and hash out our differences. It

takes time and energy to come together when we are at a crossroads of understanding or agreement, but the love in our relationship will erode over time if we ignore our feelings.

CONVERSATION STARTER

Temperaments vary, but there are times when we need to speak up, even if it is costly. Some couples may express their feelings about arguing in these ways:

Husband

I am not afraid to argue with my wife, but I am afraid of how she might react when we do argue. Sometimes it's easier not to argue and to hold what I really think inside, though occasionally it takes a while to get over my feelings. If we had more *time* to work things through, I suppose I would be more willing to open up and be honest when I really want to express my viewpoint.

Wife

I confess, I *hate* to argue! I can be quick to anger when my husband disagrees with me. I have to force myself to stay and work the issue through. My automatic tendency is to want to walk away and think whatever I want to think! We try hard to keep "issues" out in front of us and not allow them to cause a wedge between us, but it is very hard to control our emotions.

LET ME ASK YOU THIS . . .

- Do you think that arguing is healthy? Why, or why not?
- What does it mean to "fight fair"? Do you believe that we "fight fair"? What areas could we begin working on?
- Is it hard or scary for you to (potentially) argue with me? Why do you say that?

A SUGGESTED PRAYER

Father God, thank You for letting us see in Your Word that speaking out is something that needs to happen in a relationship at times. Help us to learn how to love each other *and* be honest with each other . . .

BALANCE

Unless the LORD builds the house, its builders labor in vain.
Unless the LORD watches over the city, the watchmen stand guard
in vain. In vain you rise early and stay up late, toiling for food
to eat — for he grants sleep to those he loves.

Psalm 127:1-2

S usan has always had a hard time sleeping. But lately it is getting worse. She wakes up at 2 and 3 a.m., her mind racing over the things she needs to get done.

Jeff usually falls right to sleep. Why not? He is always exhausted by the time he finally goes to bed, after having made phone calls, prepared reports, written letters, and made sure that every base was covered for the next day.

The classic "workaholic" is not so rare a species these days. I'm so often consumed with tasks and duties that I cannot function without the constant spin of the plates around me. What if they were to fall? What then?

"Unless the LORD builds the house. . . ." Do you really believe the gospel? Does it have the power to protect, guide, and lead, even when we don't? Or does God need us to constantly worry and check, check and worry to keep His world in order?

A balanced life consists of working when it's time to work, playing when it's time to play, and enjoying the gift of life as each day ends. In the frantic pace today, we lose the ability to "smell the roses." So preoccupied with the next task, our lives become busy but empty. God's desire is for us to know Him and enjoy Him forever.

"For he grants sleep to those he loves."

Because everything about our culture says, "You have to get this done!" a husband and wife may feel like this:

Husband

It is hard for me to find that very difficult line where God's responsibility stops and mine takes over, especially at work. I ask myself, *Is God* really *going to handle this, or do I need to put in a week of late nights?* But once I ask myself this question, it becomes clear that I am able to rest in the knowledge that He *does* care, but I still may have to put in some extra time. The beauty is, I don't have to carry the burden alone.

Wife

It is hard for me to know the balance of life . . . to juggle being a wife, raising children, continuing my education, working, maintaining my friendships and my growth in Christ. I often feel like I am just spinning my wheels and not doing a very good job at anything. Is there such a thing as balance in this life? I don't know.

LET ME ASK YOU THIS . . .

- What does a "balanced life" look like to you?
- Do you believe balance is a quality that can be "arrived at" in life or more a thing we all work toward and never quite master?
- Do you feel that at this point in your life you are happy with the balance you have established?
- What would you change if you could in order to feel more in control?

A SUGGESTED PRAYER

Father God, thank You for the gift of life. We confess that we move at such a frantic pace we take for granted so much You have provided to enjoy. Help us to slow down, enjoy *You*, and see the beauty and wonder around us . . .

THE BIBLE

"Heaven and earth will pass away,
but my words will never pass away."
Matthew 24:35

I t is called the Sword of the Spirit, the Holy Scriptures, and the Word of God. It has been battled, debated, chronicled, categorized, explained, defended, and debased. But the Bible has withstood it all to remain the most amazing document in human history.

Why, then, does it invite an array of negative emotions from boredom to fear in the hearts of intelligent men and women? There are the exceptions, of course: those who see the Bible as their treasured lifelong companion. But they are rare in the average pew today. Most people who profess faith in Christ spend little or no time in the Bible, with the consequence of a weakened and lethargic Christian body.

The Bible is God's direct communication to His people. His desire is to make us so keenly aware of His presence, His power, His relevance, and His love that we are able to trust Him fully. When we deny ourselves this vital lifeline, we can slip into the delusion that we know all there is to know about God—which is as frightening and arrogant as it is untrue.

Come back to the Scriptures. Read, study, and meditate on them. Renew your heart for God by the discipline of time in His Word. Like looking through an old photo album rediscovered and retrieved from your mother's attic, when reading the Bible you will find your pulse quickening over the simple beauty you have left behind.

CONVERSATION STARTER

Constantly under time pressure, a man may feel like this when it comes to reading the Bible:

Husband

There was a time when I was fascinated with the Bible. I could read for long stretches, underlining and taking notes, only to hunger for more. As my life got more complex, I allowed my practical side to justify my increasing laziness. I put reading the Bible off until I was able to find that elusive quantity called "more time." But I never will find the time unless I discipline myself to take the time.

Women often have a different approach:

Wife

The time that I spend in the Word seems to change with the particular season of life I am in. I've gone from in-depth study, to reading when I get the chance, to using the Bible as a means of going deeper with the Spirit of Christ through prayer. I appreciate how God has used the Bible in different ways to bring me to Himself.

LET ME ASK YOU THIS . . .

- How are you feeling right now about the amount of time you are spending in God's Word? If good, why? If you're dissatisfied, can you think of any options or alternatives that would help you?
- Would spending time in the Word together be a helpful thing for you? For our marriage? Would you like to commit to that sort of thing now . . . or down the road?

Dve asked several times for us to read & study together make us I feel God would more like minded

30

Father God, thank You for loving us so much that You gave us Your written Word. Thanks for the practical answers to life it addresses, and thank You for the clear simplicity of its message. Help us to be more disciplined, we confess that . . .

Our needs and thoughts would be guided by our Lord if we would ~~study~~ study together at least once a week.

Dear God. I pray, that We (Vic & myself) will someday be able to pray together openly holding each others hands. Especially at bed time when our day is finished and we tell God how we need his guidance in our lives and to bless our children and grandchild on the joy of coming together. and praising God. This is my deepest desire right now. Thank You

31

CELEBRATING OUR DIFFERENCES

The body is not made up of one part but of many.
1 Corinthians 12:14

H ave you ever taken a personality or temperament test? We have, and every time we do, we realize one thing: We are as different as night and day.

Differences are powerful. They have the ability to cement us together. We have so much to offer each other: one is an extrovert, the other an introvert; one is a conceptual thinker, the other is an intuitive feeler; one is a listener, and the other a talker. What a tremendous balance we are for each other!

Our uniqueness is also potent in how it can just as quickly drive us apart. When one wants to discuss an issue with logic, the other needs to talk about feelings. When one is frantic over schedules to keep and plans to make, the other is on the phone chatting with a friend. When the relationship needs attention, one will hide out, forcing the other to deal with the problem.

Depending on the issue, or even the timing, the differences in a marriage can make or break the relationship. But even during those times of struggle, if we see our spouse as God's gift, we can learn to celebrate our differences. When we are in need of the other's strengths it is an easy thing to praise our differences. But it is during those times of conflict that God can use our spouse in a

Let us confront our problems in God's light

Let us give each other strength!

32

way that can help us to grow.

If we are willing to work at our relationship and strive to know and understand our spouse, we will gain a greater sense of compassion for others in the process. As our love and patience for differences increase, the Body of Christ joins with us in celebrating those things that make us who we are.

"Now you are the body of Christ, and each one of you is a part of it" (1 Corinthians 12:27).

CONVERSATION STARTER

The differences between a husband and wife can bring strength to a marriage, as these paragraphs express:

Husband

During the first few years of our marriage, I found it difficult to understand my wife. She was so different. But the more I get to know her, and begin to learn from her way of looking at life, the more grateful I am for our differences. God has used her to open my eyes to so many things, that I can't imagine life without her partnership and perspective. There are those occasions, however, when I need to remind myself of how much she is a complement to me.

Many women see life more as a process, so a wife may say something like this:

Wife

I love and appreciate the qualities in my husband that are different. Yet I must admit that, because of those differences, we very often approach issues of life from opposite sides. It takes a great deal of work for us to reach a place where we can see things from the same vantage point. Ten years ago, *work* wasn't necessarily the word I would have wanted to describe my idea of marriage. But working at marriage is necessary, because it's often hard for me to see life through my husband's eyes. But every time

33

we take the time to *really* listen to each other, I realize I
wouldn't trade this relationship for *anything*! /AG 94

LET ME ASK YOU THIS . . .

- What do you see as the biggest differences between us?
- Which of our differences do you see as bringing us
  closer together? Which could (or do) tend to drive
  us apart?
- How can our differences improve our understanding
  of each other?

A SUGGESTED PRAYER

Father, thank You for making us so unique. Thank You
for the gift of our differences. We confess that sometimes
these differences tend to drive us apart, and we need Your
help to turn these tendencies around . . .

→ How we deal with Decisions
that have to be made. I like to
put them out in the open, lay
them on the table and try to find
ways to deal with them through
dialogue and questions and
research. my precious husband
seems to be scared of dealing
with lifes problems. He
likes to procrastinate and
this builds Anxiety in me
because we have to keep
going back over & over the
same problems we haven't dealt
with, therefore we are not making
progress. I like to move on
and face the challenge to grow.

34

....

CHANGE IN ME

Jesus Christ is the same yesterday and today and forever.
Hebrews 13:8

T here is only One who is consistent. The Son of God does not grow, develop, improve, or change over time. His character is constant, His love sure, His purposes definite.

Though we may dislike it and even fight it, everyone else does change. Every person we meet and every choice we make forces us to adapt and adjust. We are constantly analyzing, responding, and reacting. We sometimes change for the better, and sometimes for the worse, but we can never stay the same. Change is inevitable.

This is both the great joy and the immense challenge of living in a sinful, fallen world. For the choices we make directly impact what we become. If decisions are made out of commitment to our Lord, and to others, we develop a character that reflects those choices. But when we choose a selfish or expedient path, we become impatient and anxious in the pursuit of personal happiness.

"If anyone is in Christ, he is a new creation; the old has gone, the new has come!" (2 Corinthians 5:17).

CONVERSATION STARTERS

Because we are constantly changing, a husband may express something like this to his wife:

35

Husband

Most of the time I feel as if I am the same person who walked the halls of my high school. But a quick glance in the mirror reminds me that the years have affected me, and I am constantly changing. As I grow older, sometimes I will get confused or even blinded to the seasons of change I experience. Forgive me for those times I seem to leave you behind. But don't let me go on my own; I need you beside me throughout this process.

As she changes, a wife may want to tell her husband:

Wife

It is true that much of who I am has stayed constant, but it is important for you to know that I am not the same woman you married. As I have grown and my responsibilities have increased, the dreams and hopes within me have not lain dormant. I desire to change, to grow, and to develop my potential. Please don't be worried or threatened by this. I need your encouragement, affirmation, and help to be all that God has called me to be. I want to work with you to discover what God wants to do in and through us in the years to come. *Love Amy 9¼*

LET ME ASK YOU THIS . . .

- How are you feeling right now about the topic of change? If it is hard to describe, use single words to express your feelings.
- Are you afraid of change in me?
- How have I changed since we got married?
- Is there anything within you that you want or need to change in the next few years? If so, how can I help make that happen?

A SUGGESTED PRAYER

Father, thank You for the great adventure of life. Thank You that we never stay the same, that we are constantly growing, shifting, learning, and experiencing new things. In the midst of this, Father, we need You to remind us that as we obey You we are becoming the image of Your Son. Help us to trust You as we move through life, and help us to always seek the best for each other . .).

This is my prayer.
That we may be one in the Lord.

CHILDREN

Train a child in the way he should go,
and when he is old he will not turn from it.

Proverbs 22:6

A certain couple had three children—Robert, Sue, and Marsha. They went to church, prayed together, got along well, and were a wonderful family, almost ideal. They had "claimed" Proverbs 22:6 as the Lord's promise that their children would grow up as healthy, loving Christian kids. Everything seemed perfect.

Robert married his high school sweetheart, has a great job, and is a deacon in his church. Sue is a rising star in her company, has two kids, and actively ministers to youth. Marsha is gay, her rebelliousness borders on violence, and she wants nothing to do with the faith of her family.

The dream shattered into the anguish and pain of a family torn apart. They all were loved, they all were friends, and they all had given their lives to Christ as children. But one went her own way. She is not old—early thirties—but she shows no sign of returning to her roots.

Children are ours to protect, to teach, and to guide. We have a great deal of responsibility in how we raise them. But many in the church have read too much into that verse—they have taken the general wisdom of the proverbs and made it into a promise from God. When a child turns from God, the parents' misplaced faith leaves only a guilt-ridden alternative that points an accusing finger at them: "God didn't 'blow it,' you as *parents* obviously didn't train the child properly."

Jesus makes it very clear that the choice to follow Him is solely up to each individual. Parents, love your children, and do your best to train them in the way they should go. We will be held accountable for how we loved them. But, ultimately, they must choose for themselves the road they will take.

CONVERSATION STARTERS

Many parents worry about how their kids will turn out, and they may express their thoughts like this:

Husband

It is hard for me to avoid guilt when it comes to the kids. I think they're terrific, but there is a little voice inside me that sometimes gently reminds me of the awesome responsibility I carry as their dad. I want to be relaxed, to guide while allowing them the freedom to fail, but I am so worried that they will make poor choices, affecting the rest of their lives. It is hard to be a parent.

Wife

I think that I really do trust the Lord with the lives of my children. Yet I sometimes find that, when I sense a loss of control over what happens to them, I feel fear set in. I want so much for them to be happy and to avoid the pain I experienced growing up. I pray that the things we instill in their lives will carry them through those years of searching, but I guess there are no guarantees.

LET ME ASK YOU THIS . . .

- How do you interpret Proverbs 22:6? Are there any "guarantees" from God in raising children?
- What role did your parents play in your choice to follow Christ? Did you rebel from their models?

- What are your fears concerning our children and the choices they will make?
- Talk about how you would feel or react if one of our kids made some choices you didn't agree with and knew would be harmful.

A SUGGESTED PRAYER

Father God, You know how hard it is to raise children in this world. We love our kids and want the best for them, and we want them to know You. Help us to know the balance between loving protection and giving them room to grow. Free us from the constant worry, and help us to trust You more with the lives of our children . . .

CHURCH

Let us not give up meeting together, as some are in the habit of doing, but let us encourage one another — and all the more as you see the Day approaching.

Hebrews 10:25

Sunday morning — the day of rest, of reading the paper, of family, of leisure, and of work around the house. Oh, yes, and the ten-minute drive to church, then parking, then an hour or so in the service, some coffee, followed by the trek home. The Sunday morning ritual.

For many Christian people, church is much more than a weekly excursion to fulfill a spiritual obligation. They are involved, committed, and connected. For the vast majority of churchgoers, however, faith is limited to a semi-regular attendance at a meeting on Sunday morning. To them, church is a place to watch and mumble and sing and listen. Nothing more.

What a tragedy! The Church is the Body of Christ, and the local church is the place His people gather to worship Him, to seek His presence, counsel and comfort, and to focus on Him. It is also where we can support each other as we attempt to live our lives for Christ each day. The church is the place where we are known and we are needed. It is where we matter. For whoever follows Christ is called to a community of believers, and it takes every member in order to function properly.

Are you actively involved, or do you simply "go to

church"? God has not called us simply to sit and watch, but to gather as a community.

Because of the things he already feels responsible for, a man may state his thoughts this way:

Husband

I have been involved at church in years past, but at this point, that just doesn't seem to fit. I do have some qualities to offer (I even think I may know what my spiritual gift is), but the way our church is run, it is too draining to try to carve out a niche. It is easier to simply attend and give money.

A woman may have different feelings about church, as expressed here:

Wife

As much as I love the Lord and believe that I need to get involved at church, I must confess that it is hard for me. I have to fight against the tendency to think of reasons not to go, or to get too deeply involved. Maybe it is because I don't really feel needed or known within the supposed "family" that I don't jump right in. I serve, but with reservation.

LET ME ASK YOU THIS . . .

- How do feel about our church? Do you feel known? Needed? Valuable? Used?
- How has God equipped you to serve others, and do you take the opportunity to use those gifts?
- Do you feel we are as active as the Lord would want us to be? If we need to, how could we get more involved? Or, if we need to, how can we back off from our over-involvement?
- If God were speaking to the two of us right now,

what do you think He would say in regard to our involvement with the Body of Christ?

A Suggested Prayer

Father, thank You for the ability to worship where we want to, in the way that best fits us. We realize that many people around the world do not have that luxury. We also know that it is easy to be selfish, critical, and picky when it comes to our church. Forgive us for those ways we have hurt You by our attitudes, and help us to see how You want us to serve Your people . . .

DEATH

Death has been swallowed up in victory.
1 Corinthians 15:54

The good news of the gospel is that death has been
conquered. The sacrifice and triumph of Jesus Christ
on the cross offers to all victory over death. Herein
lies the incredible joy of Easter—we are free from the
darkest enemy we have.

Think of it: The resurrection of Jesus from the dead!
He conquered death by paying mankind's penalty so that
those who trust in Him could live forever with Him. His
gift is the promise of eternal life! We now have the promise of life better than we could even imagine. A place of
perfect peace, where there is no pain, sorrow, or tears.
A city filled with harmony, song, and love. Oh, what a
celebration awaits us when God calls us home!) 12-94

Why, then, do we fear death? What do we really have
to fear if we know that God's promises are true? Is it the
suffering? The fear of the unknown? Are we afraid for
those we leave behind?

The ultimate sting of death has been conquered, and
we are guaranteed the victory) but evil still lingers on
earth. Death was not in the mind of God when He created
us. But when we rebelled, the unnatural, painful, ugly
result was the curse of death. The stench still lingers, and
so fear remains.

We must never cease in reminding one another: "Death has been swallowed up in victory!"

CONVERSATION STARTER

Some men have a greater degree of fear than others, and may express their thoughts like this:

Husband

It is not so much death itself that I fear as it is the process leading to death. I fear the suffering, the hospitals, the waiting for test results. I am *very* afraid of being left alone if my wife were to die first, and when a movie or television show hits that nerve, I fall apart. *knew that I love you and we will be together ag..*

12-94

Some women have a different view of death, and a wife may describe what she feels like this:

Wife

The biggest issue for me is my children. I worry about their reactions and the effect it would have on their lives if my husband or I were to die. It's hard to imagine them without us. (I often long to be with Christ, but I do fear the unknown.) *12-94*

LET ME ASK YOU THIS . . .

* What about death do you fear? *the pain*
* If you could choose the way you would die and the timing, what would it be? Why? *Sudden heart attack It would be quick*
* What are some things you want to experience before you die? How can we make some of these happen? *A month vacation with my husband*

A SUGGESTED PRAYER *Praising God + loving each*

Father, whenever we are around death, it makes us con- *other* sider our own mortality. Thank You that You have promised us eternal life in Christ. We want to hold on to that hope. Help us to live our lives to the fullest, and to be free from worry about tomorrow . . . *Amen 12-94*

DISAPPOINTMENT

I am still confident of this: I will see the goodness of the LORD in the land of the living. Wait for the LORD; be strong and take heart and wait for the LORD.

Psalm 27:13-14

my prayer
12-94

T o be found lacking in a particular skill, to be evaluated and found wanting, to lose an opportunity, to receive notice saying "sorry, it fell through" — the seeds of disappointment are arrayed in a variety of shapes and colors, yet they sow a painful harvest. It is so very difficult to be turned away. But the psalmist says of God, "Be confident in Him, wait on Him, and He will give you life"!

To wait for anything has ceased to be a virtue in our day. The masses cry out for efficiency and immediate satisfaction. They are willing to wait for no one. We desire something, so we fight to get it. The *last* thing we want to hear is "wait, trust, hang in there."

Jesus Christ is alive, and He has promised us that He will win—He will defeat disappointment, anger, and sorrow. But we will never see this victory unless we are willing to wait and seek a deeper relationship with Him even in the midst of the sorrow.

Indeed, waiting can propel us into that place of which the psalmist speaks: the land of the living. For when we try to jump ahead of God, we find ourselves in bondage—relational, financial, or spiritual. But when we wait, and seek Him, there is life, there is real power for living. There we confidently find God's goodness!

CONVERSATION STARTER

With so much emphasis placed on success today, men may talk about the struggles they face like this:

Husband

When I have failed or been let down by people or circumstances beyond my control, I feel disappointed, but I try not to think about it. One of my biggest fears is being out of control, and disappointments often scare me to death. To be so convinced that God is in control and that I can simply "wait" for Him stretches my ability to trust.

Women may face a different set of circumstances, but their disappoints are just as real. Many may feel this way:

Wife

Disappointment hits hardest when I feel taken for granted, misrepresented, or manipulated. Because these are so intangible, often it is difficult for me to identify them, much less express them. I usually try to appear strong, so I suppress my emotions, but I remain in their grasp until I can find the courage to admit my pain to others, especially the Lord. *Amy 94*

LET ME ASK YOU THIS ...

- Describe the last time you felt disappointed. What caused it? *Not being able to discuss things openly.*
- How did you respond? *In anger.*
- Have I caused you disappointment lately?

A SUGGESTED PRAYER

Father, as we have talked we realize that we get discouraged and disappointed more often than we like to admit. Help us to come to You and each other when we are hurt or frustrated by failure or circumstances. Free us to trust You, even when things don't go the way we want them to ... *Amen*

DREAMS

*"I will pour out my Spirit on all people. Your sons
and daughters will prophesy, your old men will dream dreams,
your young men will see visions."*

Joel 2:28

A homemaker who sits alone surrounded by needy children . . . a businessman who is lonely and unfulfilled at the office . . . a retired couple who faithfully attend church but can't seem to find their niche. . . .

Is there ever a time to stop dreaming?

For many, the struggle with today's responsibilities makes us believe that we don't have the time or energy to think about tomorrow's dreams. Jesus did say, "Do not worry about tomorrow, for tomorrow will worry about itself" (Matthew 6:34), but there must be a distinction between needless fretting due to a lack of faith and worthwhile dreaming of dreams. The Lord never intended for us to allow our world to keep us from praying, thinking, planning, and dreaming about the future.

The mission of Jesus Christ is to bring hope to the burdened and freedom to the captive. There is no circumstance that can shackle the one who is in relationship to Him. Though we may feel everyday pressures squeezing us to the point of panic and despair, there is always hope. Jesus' determined control over the circumstances of our lives and His promise of guidance and fulfillment give us the confidence to dream.

Do you harbor a hidden dream? In Jesus Christ hide

no more. Throw open the doors and shout it to the world. "The LORD delights in those who fear him, who put their hope in his unfailing love" (Psalm 147:11).

In a world filled with worry and struggle, a man may express his desire to dream like this:

Husband
Usually I am too busy to dream. At other times I am too frightened, for dreaming might mean a change, and the older I get the harder it is to contemplate change. But sometimes, when I let myself go, I can see a long-suppressed desire begin to blossom, and as a result I find myself excited about the possibility of my dream unfurled. Can I dream without worry? I want to, I really want to!

Obligations, expectations, and responsibilities may keep a woman from dreaming, but her heart may want to cry out:

Wife
For me dreaming is an issue of time. When a friend asks, "How are you?" often I am unable to answer because my day has been too full to even ask myself that question. Dream . . . it is what my heart yearns to do. I hope I will not forget how before this season of young children passes.

LET ME ASK YOU THIS . . .
- When you were a child, what did you want to be when you grew up? *I always wanted to be able to spend a lot of time getting to know the Lord.*
- If money and circumstances were not an issue, is there anything that you would love to do? *To minister to*
- Do you have any dreams, hidden or not, that you *hurting people.*

49

might want to pursue? What can I do to help you realize these dreams?

A SUGGESTED PRAYER

Father, grant us the courage to be as little children—to dream dreams, to hope for new horizons. Free us from what binds us in the present and help us to follow whatever call we sense . . .

My dream would be to minister to my sisters and then family to tell them of the Love and peace they can have by accepting Jesus Christ as Lord of their lives. The Love we should have for each other. that what we have here on earth will pass away but our love will last all eternity. That trying to care for our parents is noble and good and to support each other, to make it loving and a kind thing, not a power struggle. To shower love on our parents in their last days, to let Gods love shine through   12-94
I have made many mistakes
Please forgive me

DUTY OF DEVOTION

"I no longer call you servants, because a servant does not know his master's business. Instead, I have called you friends, for everything that I learned from my Father I have made known to you."
John 15:15

A mong many who claim to be followers of Jesus Christ, Christian devotion has been relegated to a duty. It's a noble duty, but one more obligation to be fulfilled, nonetheless. As such, it is just one of many such essential and noble duties — family, marriage, career. We may rationalize, "Even though I know my relationship with God is important, He understands how pulled and stretched I am." The result? Often one of two extremes — a lackluster faith with little power, or guilt because of what we're *not* doing.

Loving Jesus is not a responsibility to be fulfilled, it is an invitation to a dynamic relationship. His invitation is to learn from Him, to know Him and follow Him. Only when there is a realization that loving and knowing Jesus is what brings stability, meaning, health, and direction to every facet of life's concerns can we be free from the stress of obligation.

Jesus said, "If anyone would come after me, he must deny himself and take up his cross daily and follow me" (Luke 9:23). How would anyone who heard Jesus talk of such commitment and devotion react to our fragmented understanding of the Christian life? When Jesus called us His friends, He called us to a much deeper relationship

51

than could ever be seen as a "duty." To know, trust, and love my spouse is not merely my duty, it is my pledge, formed in love and cultivated by experience. Does the Lord deserve any less?

CONVERSATION STARTER

The words of Jesus are enticingly demanding, but the reality of living them is another matter that may be expressed this way:

Husband

I *want* to follow Jesus, I really do, but I have almost given up trying to walk the tightrope between being a devoted Christian and keeping the rest of my life in order. As I say this, I am aware that it boils down to this question: Is my faith for real and my desire to follow Jesus rooted in a relationship with Him, or am I living a spiritual charade? If I *truly* desire Jesus Christ as my Lord and my friend, my response to spending time with Him in prayer and His Word would be clearer. That is the choice I face, and I make that choice daily, one way or another.

Wife

I think that Jesus is more concerned about turning my heart toward Him than He is about what my devotional time looks like. It is easy to get caught up in Christianity's "rule book" and constantly feel guilty for what I am or am *not* doing, and lose focus on the object of my faith.

LET ME ASK YOU THIS . . .

- In *one word*, describe your relationship with Jesus right now. Why did you choose that word? Do you believe that He is pleased with your relationship? Are you?
- What do you think God expects of you in terms of your devotion and commitment to Him? How do you know?

ఇ If you were to change one thing about your life—
schedule, attitude, habits, lifestyle, etc.—what would
it be? How can we change that together?

ఇ Name one believer you know personally whose heart
for Christ and lifestyle you admire. What about that
person draws you? Would it be appropriate to ask
him or her for advice and counsel for your own spiritual journey? How can I help you take that step?

A SUGGESTED PRAYER

Our Father, we confess that we have not loved You with
our whole heart, soul, mind, and strength. We want to
follow You, but we need Your guidance and grace to know
the balance it takes to follow You today. Help us to place
You at the center of our lives, and teach us to see everything we do from Your perspective . . .

ENCOURAGEMENT

Encourage one another daily, as long as it is called Today,
so that none of you may be hardened by sin's deceitfulness.
Hebrews 3:13

The surest antidote in the battle against the powers of darkness is a regular dose of encouragement. When I am convinced that I'm on my own, where no one believes in or cares for me, I often feel forced to look inward. As the process of self-interest and self-preservation continues I am deceived into thinking that I am free and need no one. The cycle continues until it produces a cold heart whose selfishness has become hardened beyond repair. The deceit is complete; the battle lost.

Encouragement is a valuable and necessary gift we are called to provide others daily. To remind others of their infinite worth and value, to call them to deeper relationships, to inspire them to press on in their faith reminds them that someone cares. As we are continually softened by the input of those who love us, it is impossible for sin's deceitfulness to get a foothold.

"Encourage one another daily."

CONVERSATION STARTER

Because success and productivity are the values of the day, we find little time for honest encouragement. Some men may express their thoughts like this:

Husband

I like to think that I am an encouraging person—that I give credit where credit is due, and a pat on the back for a job well done. But am I good at encouraging others so that they know I care about them? I think not. Most of my encouragement is tied to performance, and it is unusual for me to encourage someone just to keep them going.

A woman may see encouragement in a different way:

Wife

When I receive encouragement I no longer feel the need to protect myself. I feel good about who I am, which frees me to encourage others. I wish my ability to give was not so tied to people, but rather to knowing that the Lord cares for me as I am.

LET ME ASK YOU THIS . . .

- List three people who encourage you. What qualities in them give you this impression? How do they specifically encourage you?
- What is the best way I can encourage you?
- What person needs your encouragement this week? What specific steps can you take to help that person?

A SUGGESTED PRAYER

Heavenly Father, thank You that You are the Great Encourager. Thank You that You want us to know how much You care for us despite our weaknesses and failures. Help us to be less worried about how much encouragement we need and focus on encouraging others . . .

ENVY

For where you have envy and selfish ambition,
there you find disorder and every evil practice.
But the wisdom that comes from heaven is first of all pure;
then peace-loving, considerate, submissive,
full of mercy and good fruit, impartial and sincere.
James 3:16-17

There is no way around it—envy is evil. We toss the word around with such ease, such flippancy, that it has lost its power and its sting. But envy hurts everything it touches.

To allow envy to infest a marriage is to drive a wedge between the very fibers of the relationship. The Bible equates envy with "selfish ambition." Thus the one who harbors a spirit of envy is no longer concerned with what they can give to the relationship because they are so preoccupied with what they can grab. When one seeks his or her own interests at the expense of the spouse, often the other will feel forced to retaliate.

The primary antidote for this hopeless situation—where the vicious cycle repeats itself until there is deep division—is godly wisdom.

Be careful not to let envy or selfish ambition gain a foothold in your relationship. But if it does, actively pursue the wise counsel of the Lord. In approaching God together you will find His help. God may choose to guide you through other people, or the Scriptures, or prayer. As you resist the temptation of envy, God will give you the resources to fight this enemy that comes to divide your marriage.

In a culture that takes envy so lightly, some men may allow themselves to fall into the trap of complaining about the inequity of marriage roles, as expressed like this:

Husband
Though "envy" seems a little strong, there are times when I find myself feeling a twinge of jealousy toward my wife. Whether it is her friendships, schedule, or mood, I want what she has. Even if I don't say anything, when I let myself dwell on what *I* want, I resent her all the more. Eventually it all comes out anyway, and we argue over whose life is easier, better, or more desirable. When we get in this trap, we both lose.

Many women may have a different kind of struggle, as this opinion expresses:

Wife
I have felt envious of the opportunity my husband has had to realize his dreams. There have been times when I have wanted to be seen as an individual who has value on my own, not just as "his wife." Although this struggle is difficult, it has turned out to be a gift in my life, teaching me the lesson of finding my true identity in Christ alone.

LET ME ASK YOU THIS . . .

- What do you think it means to "envy"? How do you feel about envy?
- Where have you harbored a sense of envy toward someone recently? Describe it. Do you still feel this way?
- Is there anything you need to do or change to be more personally fulfilled and less prone to envy or jealousy?

A Suggested Prayer

Father, thank You for Your promise to care for each of us as individuals. We confess that we at times look at others and want what they have. This causes us to lose faith in Your provision and affects our ability to love them. Please grant us the faith to be satisfied and secure with who we are and what we have . . .

EVANGELISM

"Therefore go and make disciples of all nations."
Matthew 28:19

I n college, a friend whom I had been talking to about Jesus was asked by an unknown student to respond to a survey on religion. My friend was just beginning to show an interest in spiritual things, so he decided to help the student out. He answered each question as diligently as he could. When he got to the end of the questionnaire, he found a question asking if he wanted to "accept Jesus into his heart." My friend felt used and manipulated. He was deeply offended at the tactic of this stranger and (in his words) the way he "tried to shove Jesus down my throat!" As he walked away, he walked away from Jesus Christ as well.

Some people may feel that, though harsh, the direct approach is the best method of evangelism; there are going to be those who reject the truth, and that is the way it goes. Others, however, are probably shocked to hear of such a "hard sell" in the name of Jesus. Wouldn't love, kindness, and friendship have won the heart of this student, given time? When Jesus tells every believer to "go and make disciples," what method does He want us to use in bringing people to the truth? There are so many options, and each uses the Bible for justification. How does Christ want us to put His gospel into action?

In light of the disagreements, that may be the wrong question. What matters to God is not so much the method as the motive. Is your heart broken for those who don't know Christ? Are you willing to sacrifice to see that others get a clear, uncluttered hearing? When praying for family, friends, neighbors, and coworkers, do you ask for opportunities to somehow bring them before Jesus? This is the call of every Christian: bring the light of Jesus to a world filled with darkness.

> How, then, can they [unbelievers] call on the one they have not believed in? And how can they believe in the one of whom they have not heard? And how can they hear without someone preaching to them? (Romans 10:14)

CONVERSATION STARTER

Because of the many methods of evangelism, men often leave it up to the experts, as described this way:

Husband

When I first became a Christian I was actively concerned that everyone around me would come to know Jesus. But frankly, as I've grown older, it doesn't even cross my mind much. I have the ability to "tune out" those messages I have heard over and over, and my responsibility to the "lost" seems to be in that category. I *know* that there are people all around me who need Christ, but I subconsciously avoid having to get involved.

A woman may have a different perspective, as expressed here:

Wife

I believe that the best way to bring someone to Christ is by loving them first, "Winning the right to be heard." I have felt that as long as I am growing in my knowledge

and love for Christ then His life in me would be visible
to others. But, there are other times when I question my
witness for Him and wonder if I am verbally bold enough.
I am not always sure what the "right" balance is, and
so when I err it is usually on the cautious side. But is
that best?

LET ME ASK YOU THIS . . .

- When you consider the Bible's call to "go into all
  the world" with the gospel, what are some words to
  describe your thoughts?
- Tell me again how you came to know Christ. Was
  there an individual who especially touched you? Was
  there a particular method, speaker, or program that
  made a difference?
- In what ways do you think God wants you involved
  in reaching out to others right now? Is there something we can do as a couple?
- Who are some people God may want you (or us) to
  reach out to with the love of Christ?

A SUGGESTED PRAYER

Father, thank You for loving us and for bringing Your
truth into our lives. Give us compassion for those who
don't know You. Help us to be obedient to You by sharing
the gospel with them, as we pray for them by name . . .

FAILURE

At my first defense, no one came to my support,
but everyone deserted me.

2 Timothy 4:16

T here is no venture, no contest, no endeavor that seeks as its end to fail. But failures happen — regularly.

In today's world where efficiency is valued above character, we often view failure as unacceptable. We have been raised with a culturally imposed belief in measurable success. We come to believe that anything less than success will be devastating to our future. A failure triggers a painful inner alarm, and we begin to question our inherent value and worth. We have not only hurt ourselves and our future, we have let others down.

In many cultures, however, failure is seen as a natural byproduct of education. In much of the Third World the process of growth is far more valued than the final product. In Western culture, however, the pressure to succeed runs deep.

When we fail, we must seek to learn from our failures, and not be so crushed that we are paralyzed emotionally. We have to grow to the place where we are able to adjust, reattempt, and move on. Our worth is not diminished, our identity not destroyed.

Seldom do we have the courage to learn from our failures. In the realm of relationships, especially marriage, we need to constantly move toward the goal of seeing failure as a learning experience.

From today's standpoint, the Apostle Paul died a failure. The above verse refers to his loneliness while on trial as a believer. But with God's unconditional love as his foundation, he didn't allow the disappointment of apparent failure to daunt him. He knew that ultimately he was loved, and therefore *it was safe to fail*. Don't be so hard on yourself that you cannot receive and experience the grace of God.

CONVERSATION STARTER

To be viewed as a failure is devastating for a man, and in the context of marriage some men may express this fear:

Husband

I know I will let my wife down. At some point, I will disappoint her, discourage her, and discount her worth. But if I begin to see myself as a failure because of these missteps, I might be irreparably crushed. I need my wife and close friends to give me the grace it takes to learn from my mistakes as I figure out how to love her as God instructs me to.

A woman may talk about her perspective on personal failure this way:

Wife

Failure is something I am not comfortable with. When I fail, it is hard for me to maintain a sense of self-worth, realizing it doesn't change the fact that I am valuable in God's eyes. Often I struggle to accept love and the freedom to fail, regardless of how mundane or how critical my failure might be.

LET ME ASK YOU THIS . . .

❧ What is the most devastating failure you have experienced? Describe what happened and how it felt. Do you feel that you are healed of the pain?

❧ Where in the last few months have I failed you, however slightly? What could I have done to have avoided it? Have you forgiven me? Are you over it?

A SUGGESTED PRAYER

Father, thank You that our failures have been wiped away by Your love as expressed through Your Son's sacrifice on the cross. Free us from the guilt of past failures, and teach us through the consequences of tomorrow's . . .

FAITH

"Look at the nations and watch — and be utterly amazed.
For I am going to do something in your days
that you would not believe, even if you were told."

Habakkuk 1:5

C hildren gaze at the fireplace on Christmas Eve, wondering how Santa could possibly fit down the chimney. There is no doubt in their minds that the jolly old elf manages this feat, even as they ask a myriad of questions laced with wonder and amazement. Santa is Santa, and they know that he comes down chimneys — what a wonder!

As adults we know better. There is no Santa, no Easter Bunny, no "Man in the Moon." We are eminently rational, teetering on the edge of the cynical. Whatever we can measure and predict with certainty is true, outside of that we are skeptical at best.

Only a remnant say that God remains a mystery, a wonder, and a surprise to anyone who will risk. He has always been in the business of throwing the unexpected curveball to His creatures. It is not God's fault that little wonder remains in the world. He has never stopped working, intervening, pursuing, and directing. People have just stopped looking. Childlike faith has given way to an overwrought scientific rationalism. Faith and mystery are relegated to a tiny corner of life.

Remember, "Without faith it is impossible to please God" (Hebrews 11:6).

In our world of experts and specialists, it is little wonder that childlike faith is rare, causing many a man to put his feelings like this:

Husband

I know the Bible stories that tell us of God's miraculous power, and I basically believe that they are true. But when I am confronted with the need for a similar faith here and now, I tend to dismiss the possibility. I have been so conditioned by my world that I rarely even give the miraculous power of God much thought. It is revolutionary to think that He still acts with power in our day-to-day affairs.

For women, faith often has a different feel, and may be expressed this way:

Wife

Faith for me is easy when life's circumstances are under control. But when opportunities come where God asks me to walk by faith, the test can be unnerving. In times like these, my faith is more a cry, "Help, Lord! I need You!" I don't really like the process, but it is when I am at that point that I begin to experience God's power, and my faith grows.

LET ME ASK YOU THIS ...

- What is one situation when you had a hard time looking to God in faith? What caused you to doubt?
- Are there any areas of life (family, parenting, work, leisure, etc.) that you have allowed to stand apart from your faith in God? If so, why?
- On a scale of 1-10 (10 being Mother Teresa) how much faith do you have in God to act in a miraculous way, and why?

A SUGGESTED PRAYER

Our Father, thank You for letting us see Your power and compassion in Your Word. Remind us that You never change, and You are still as interested in Your people as You were in biblical days. Grant us the faith to trust You to lead, protect, and act on our behalf—in every area of our lives . . .

FEAR

David said to Saul, "Let no one lose heart on account of this Philistine; your servant will go and fight him."

1 Samuel 17:32

The sheer arrogance of David — a mere shepherd boy among experienced warriors. For any rational person, facing the giant was suicide; who could beat this Goliath? While the enemy repeated his taunts and jeers to the armies of the living God, the soldiers were paralyzed with fear. Who could possibly silence such a towering foe?

A young boy armed only with five stones and an unshakable, seemingly irrational faith in his God met the challenge. Even the king's armor and bronze helmet he rejected, for those tools of war did not suit David. He was a shepherd boy, but he was not afraid because he knew Him who knows no fear. And his decisive victory made history.

Israel's fear of Goliath exemplifies the uncertainty and emotional paralysis that can invade our lives. A giant stands before us, shouting insults and mocking the power of our God. Where is the One behind the shepherd boy turned king when we need Him? He is with us, and He is armed with the authority to defeat the powers arrayed against us. His name is Jesus Christ.

Be certain of this: "From the LORD comes deliverance" (Psalm 3:8).

CONVERSATION STARTER

Though uncomfortable to acknowledge and discuss, at one time or another fear is a very real issue for men. Some may express their feelings about fear like this:

Husband

I learned at an early age that a man was expected to accept his fears and face them head on. With most of those things I fear I am able to swallow hard, put on an air of confidence, and press on. But there are times when I am afraid — no matter how I try to act — and I don't know how to handle that.

A woman may keep her feelings closer to the surface. Social mores have given her permission to fear, and it's possible that she is further down the road to peace. She might express it like this:

Wife

Fear, panic, chaos — my mind races with "What if?" I pick up the phone and call every friend I can think of who might be able to offer a word of wisdom or comfort. Sometimes the Lord speaks through them, but usually I hang up feeling empty and afraid. Well, maybe it is time to hit my knees. I've exhausted human resources and remain in need. So after all my effort, I finally admit, "Okay, Lord, it's You and me."

LET ME ASK YOU THIS . . .

- 🍃 Can you describe the most fearful thing you have faced in your lifetime? Tell me five words that best characterize the feelings you had when you faced this fear.
- 🍃 What were your sources of comfort during this time?
- 🍃 How did God enter into your response to fear? Was your relationship to Him different as a result?
- 🍃 Is there anything you fear now? Do you ever fear me?

A Suggested Prayer

Father, during the dark days when we feel oppression and confusion and are afraid, grant us the faith to look to You for strength and comfort. Help us to see that when we fear You as the mighty Lord and King, You promise to be our refuge, and nothing can harm us beyond what You give us strength to bear . . .

FORGIVENESS

"Lord, how many times shall I forgive my brother
when he sins against me? Up to seven times?"
Jesus answered, "I tell you, not seven times,
but seventy-seven times."
Matthew 18:21-22

The basis of forgiveness is rooted not only in God's justice, but also in identification with Christ. Our natural tendency when wronged or hurt is to seek justice and retribution. Our sense of justice has been violated; we want someone to pay. But when we stand as the accused, we plead for mercy, understanding, and grace.

Before the dawn of time Jesus chose to forgive believers of every deed and thought that runs contrary to His law of love. Our sin runs deep, but the mercy of God's forgiveness goes deeper. We hurt others, for our selfishness destroys relationships. We deny our God, yet He forgives. We remain His delight because the love He expressed on the cross brings us before Him in robes "whiter than snow."

Now that we have been forgiven, Jesus expects us to extend His mercy to everyone we encounter. Nothing they do will ever be any worse than we ourselves have done. In the presence of Goodness, we all stand together in need of mercy.

As we talk about forgiveness, we remember that God's Word says, "There is no one righteous, not even one" (Romans 3:10).

Forgiveness may be easy to talk about, but most men find it difficult to do, as expressed here:

Husband

I can forgive someone who seeks forgiveness, or who at least appears contrite. I have a hard time with those who either don't care that they have wronged someone (especially me!) or who are oblivious. But when I don't forgive I can't seem to shake my anger and bitterness. I usually resign myself that I don't like that so-and-so and they don't deserve my regard. By allowing myself to think this way I place myself above them. I know this is wrong and I must do something about my attitude.

Most women also have a hard time forgiving others, as represented by this opinion:

Wife

It is relatively easy for me to forgive outwardly. But inwardly, where I must completely let go of it, that is a different thing for me. It is easy for me to harbor anger and mistrust in my heart, to dwell on it and allow it to cloud how I love the person who has wronged me. But I know that ultimately I am the one who suffers most. I find that when I hold on to these feelings I block myself from experiencing God's peace.

LET ME ASK YOU THIS . . .

- ᴥ Can you name two people over the past few years whom you have had a hard time forgiving? What were the circumstances?
- ᴥ Are you still holding on to your feelings, or have you moved on? Are you able to freely care for them now?
- ᴥ What are some ways we can help each other grow in forgiveness?

A SUGGESTED PRAYER

Father, we believe that You are right when You tell us to freely forgive, for we know that we are no better than those who hurt us. Forgive us for striking back at them by not letting go of the offense in our hearts. Help us to humbly see ourselves as You see us—broken, hurting people who have been healed by the love of Christ . . .

•••

FRIENDS

Recalling your tears, I long to see you,
so that I may be filled with joy.
2 Timothy 1:4

As busy as we get these days, our lives are never so full as to not need friends. We may be motivated by money, success, advancement, or achievement, but we are *touched* by friendship. We are never so rich as when we love and are loved by a friend.

But friendship that means anything is never realized without cost and sacrifice. To know someone takes an enormous investment of time, usually time that we don't really have. Routines may have to change, and roles may have to be redefined. Although the cost may be high, the cultivation of a friendship is the secret to the joy of life.

Parents who are too busy with their children or who haven't the energy to spend with others in a meaningful, relaxed way will wonder why they are so often lonely. Even in the best marriages, a couple who has not sought opportunities for time and depth with other couples will eventually find themselves isolated.

Give yourself away to a friend. Your reward will be rich indeed.

CONVERSATION STARTER

For many men, friendships are actually no more than casual acquaintances, as some men may express:

Husband

I know a lot of people, and I consider most of them friends. But my responsibilities at work, at home and at church leave me little time for "hanging out." Even if I had the time, I'm not sure what we would talk about other than business and sports, and that could get old fast. I do wish, however, I had a few friendships where I could cut loose and be myself.

Some women, on the other hand, can be completely absorbed in their friendships, as expressed here:

Wife

I don't know what I would do without my friends. There are a few that God has brought into my life with whom I can experience the joy of being known and loved for who I am, totally apart from the roles I play. With these friends I find safety, trust, perspective, support, and encouragement. It is scary to think about who I would be today without the blessing of their presence in my life over the years.

LET ME ASK YOU THIS . . .

- ❧ Who are some of your closest friends? What is it about these relationships that you appreciate? Does your schedule reflect your commitment to them? How can I help you deepen these friendships even more?
- ❧ Is there a relationship that you don't feel really great about in your life right now? What do you think God would want you to do? What could we pray together for that relationship—for the Lord's reconciliation or leading in it?
- ❧ How can we deepen our friendship with those couples we consider our closest friends?

A SUGGESTED PRAYER

Father, thank You for the gift of friends. It is hard for us to find enough time to give to our friends. Help us to balance our lives and schedules to enable us to enjoy our friendships . . .

FUN

Live as children of the light.

Ephesians 5:8

People have forgotten how to have fun. As one writer put it, we are no longer travelers walking down the road of life. We have become harried tourists on the constant edge of boredom, with our sunglasses, video cameras and checkbooks, hurrying to the next exhibit that grabs our attention. Soon we lose interest and move on to something else that demands nothing more of us than a vague attraction. In life's grand adventure we have lost the drive of the participant, and have clung to the mindless comfort of the fan.

But to "live as children of the light" we are invited to recapture the joy of living. If you know Christ your zest for the journey should come as naturally as breathing. His love frees us of the need to pretend and the nagging anxiety of everyday demands.

Laugh, Christian; run, tickle, sing, play! Sound the horn and dance. Challenge your children to play freeze tag, fly a kite, climb a tree.

You are loved, you are free—*rejoice!*

CONVERSATION STARTER

In thinking about what it means to experience the joy of living, many men may say:

Husband

Because much of my life is consumed with the burden of responsibility, I tend to think more in terms of finding time to rest than of letting loose and having fun. Activities I do now and then help me relax, but I would not call them fun exactly. It is hard for me to let my relationship with God free me to the point that I see my life as a "grand adventure."

As women consider how to "live as children of the light," they may express their feelings this way:

Wife

I have always considered myself to be a fun, spontaneous person. But something last week caused me to reevaluate. My nine-year-old son couldn't find anyone to play him in air hockey, so I volunteered. He was incredulous! He turned to me with surprise on his face and replied, "*You* want to play, Mom?" I shot back, "Why does that surprise you? I'm a fun person!" He just stared at me.

LET ME ASK YOU THIS . . .

- Describe the most fun you had as a child. What ingredients made it fun?
- Define "fun." Is this word limited to childrens' activities or is it for us, too? What would fun look like for an adult?
- What are three fun things that you would like to do with me?

A SUGGESTED PRAYER

Father, we confess that in many ways we have forgotten how to have fun. We have let the joy of life become abstract, and we are too preoccupied with the "serious" affairs of life. Help us to recapture a childhood flair for life, and to see each day as an opportunity to experience Your joy in a new way . . .

GIFTS

"Stop bringing meaningless offerings!
Your incense is detestable to me."

Isaiah 1:13

"It's not the gift, it's the thought that counts." This poetic, almost trite sentiment has few supporters when they are the recipient of a gift. The proverbial Christmas fruitcake, for example, is usually delivered and received graciously. But it is just as often the first thing thrown out the day after Christmas. We justify this mysterious ritual without noticing that no more thought was given to its demise than to its purchase. It has become a meaningless gift!

Is the Lord saying to His people that He expects *no gifts* from them? Of course not. The expression of a loving and grateful heart is giving. He *is* saying that giving a *meaningless* gift is worse than no gift at all. Incense without humility and service is "detestable" (a very strong word indeed!) to Him. Don't give Him the incense, Israel, unless it is given *from the heart.*

Sometimes the best way to show someone we care is to offer a gift. It doesn't have to be expensive, but it must be costly. It requires compassion as its driving force, and its aim is to say, "You are important to me." So give the one you love a gift—a song, a poem, or a night off. But beware the offhand or grudging gift, for they are no less offensive than incense when given out of a sense of obligation. The thought and passion that motivate the giver is what brings value to the gift.

When searching for ways to show his love for his wife, a man may say:

Husband
When my wife and I were dating it was easy to find creative ways to express my feelings, for I could think about little else but her. The longer we're together, I find I'm less inclined to be creative but, ironically, much more in love. When we *do* try to be spontaneous and creative it really brings us together. That is one way we keep some spark in our relationship.

When thinking about giving and getting gifts, a woman may say something like this:

Wife
I love surprises! To me they keep wonder and spontaneity alive in a relationship. Consequently, birthdays and holidays are major occasions for me. The trap that I need to be careful of, however, is letting my expectations get the better of me (especially if I haven't communicated them). It is easy for me to feel let down and disappointed. I will never forget the Mother's Day when my sweet husband and son excitedly handed me their present. I burst out in tears when I opened the gift—they had bought me a Dustbuster!

LET ME ASK YOU THIS . . .
- What is the greatest gift you have ever received? The worst?
- What is the most memorable gift you have received from me?
- Do you feel that I do enough to show my love and

appreciation for you? What are some ways that you can help me in this?

A SUGGESTED PRAYER

Father, we are so grateful for the relationship that You have given us. Though we may not express it very well, we know how blessed we are. Help us to surprise each other with gifts . . .

GROWING OLDER

All our days pass away under your [the Lord's] wrath; we finish our years with a moan. The length of our days is seventy years — or eighty, if we have the strength; yet their span is but trouble and sorrow, for they quickly pass, and we fly away.

Psalm 90:9-10, A prayer of Moses

Our culture seeks to perfect the art of hiding the pain, loneliness, and rejection of old age. We are so ashamed of the helplessness aging brings that we sanitize our lives by locking away those who remind us of our mortality. To a lot of folks, old age is a curse to be avoided as long as possible.

In this psalm, Moses seems to agree with this depressing sentiment. What are the aged good for, anyway? When we are old, we lose our productivity, our reasoning, even our ability to care for ourselves. Perhaps this is why the aged are shoved aside, neatly tucked away, so as not to depress anyone with their plight.

But, wait and see how the psalm unfolds! The Lord *does* have compassion, and when we are old, He has more compassion still! The Lord hears our cry: "Satisfy us in the morning with your unfailing love, that we may sing for joy and be glad all our days" (Psalm 90:14). Even in our old age, Jesus Christ will make us sing, for we are His!

Oh, how wrong we are to flee the great truth of life. With the exception of a few, we will all grow old. As we do, we must continue to fight the temptation to buy into the lie that we have no worth, no meaning, no dignity. We are His, and we can sing it with joy!

Depending on age and family history, many men may feel like this when it comes to thinking of growing older:

Husband
It scares me to think that when I grow old I will no longer be able to take care of myself. I have a hard time even being around elderly people, and yet I know I should have compassion on them. Maybe my own fear of aging has caused me to want to ignore them.

Many women, who are closer to their families, may say:

Wife
The greatest hero in my life was my grandma. She was in her seventies when she died, but I will never saw her as old. She had so much life, so much joy. Even when she was sick, there was a sparkle and a love for Jesus that made her glow. I never forget her. She is my model of aging: for her every day was an adventure and another opportunity to bring some light and happiness to others. I hope it will be that way for me.

LET ME ASK YOU THIS . . .

ᨠ How do you feel about the elderly? What are some words to describe your feelings? Why doesn't society think of old age as the "golden years" anymore?

ᨠ How do you feel about growing older? Are you frightened? Why do you feel the way you do?

ᨠ How does God want us to treat the elderly in our church and community? Is there anything specific we could do to help them see their worth?

A SUGGESTED PRAYER

Lord Jesus, You understand what we feel when we are lonely, afraid, and in need of others. We confess that it is hard at this stage of our lives to think about growing older. Help us to have compassion on our elders . . .

HEALING

The word of the LORD came to him [Isaiah]: "Go back and tell Hezekiah, the leader of my people, 'This is what the LORD, the God of your father David, says: I have heard your prayer and seen your tears; I will heal you.'"

2 Kings 20:4-5

H ezekiah was one of the greatest kings in Israel's history. We are told that "there was no one like him among all the kings of Judah, either before him or after him" (2 Kings 18:5). When Hezekiah was very ill, the Lord declared that his time was up. But the faithful king prayed for deliverance, and God responded not only by healing him, but also by adding fifteen years to his life.

Some Christians teach that God doesn't heal anymore, others that He will heal only *occasionally*, and never because of someone's gift of healing. Still others believe that God *always* heals in response to faith, for as James 5:15 states, "The prayer offered in faith will make the sick person well." Where is the truth? Did God formerly care personally for His people, but now has He left us to modern medicine? Or is He harder to reach today, demanding that His people jump through numerous "hoops" of faith in order to receive healing?

That debate has raged for two millennia, and it will continue, for it is one of those issues that cannot be neatly systematized. But there are two things we can count on: First, Jesus loves us; second, He is able to heal us. His healing may not always fit our agenda, or look the way we want it to, but He is faithful to those He loves, and we can trust Him.

Where do you need His healing touch?

CONVERSATION STARTER

Because men tend to be more pragmatic, many may express their feelings about healing like this:

Husband

I figure that God has given us medical science because He wants us to use His gift of creation in the healing process. But when a doctor can't "fix it," I become disturbed, and sometimes my faith gets a little shaken. I *want* to believe in divine healing. I just don't understand why God seems so distant and impotent in times of severe pain and hardship. Maybe it is this that keeps me from praying with conviction and looking for Him to heal even my little hurts. But I *do* believe in His power and love.

Many women may feel more deeply about healing, and may express their thoughts like this:

Wife

The healing of God is a confusing issue for me. I do not understand why He chooses to show Himself in miraculous ways to some and apparently remain silent with others. I feel like I know the heart of Jesus enough to trust that He *desires* to make whole each and every one of His children and has the power to do so. Yet there are things I will have to ask Him when we are face to face, like, "Why, Lord, didn't You heal my friend?"

LET ME ASK YOU THIS . . .

🐦 Have you ever wrestled with God over the issue of healing? If so, how?

🐦 Has there been someone who needed healing, and whom you prayed for, yet God seemed to remain silent? Tell me about it. Describe how you felt toward Him.

🖙 Do you feel clean with the Lord now or does that issue (or others like it) cause some skepticism or mistrust in your relationship with Jesus?

🖙 Where do you need the Lord's healing touch? How can we help each other have a greater sense of faith and expectancy?

A SUGGESTED PRAYER

Father, this issue is so difficult for us. We over-spiritualize Your ability to heal, and yet You clearly healed many when You lived on earth. Help us not to stop praying, or stop trusting You . . .

HOPE

"Nothing is impossible with God."
Luke 1:37

When your little girl is hurt, she is easily comforted resting in the arms of her mother. Worry is wiped away, for Mommy will make everything "all better."

We live within the tension of extremes. On the one hand, it is easy to hold a pessimistic view of the world: economic uncertainties, family instability, military oppression and conflict, cancer, AIDS, worry, tension, stress. But at the same time, optimism abounds in our world. There remains an almost naive faith in this highly uncertain "world community" — a belief in a "new world order." The more we watch the news, the more we are subject to tremendous emotional swings from one extreme to the other.

But for the Christian there is only one world view — the certainty of hope. No matter how dark, oppressive, or lonely the present may be, those in Christ know that they will triumph. Through compassion and power He is eternally committed to our lost and hurting world. Jesus will never stand on the sidelines, waiting for us. His promises bring hope, and His character demands that He act.

Give Him your anxiety, your heartache, your uncertainties. Trust Him to hold you close, and allow your optimism to rest not on the achievement of people but on the certainty of His character.

In a world that can't decide which is more fitting, gloom or optimism, a man might express his thoughts this way:

Husband

It is easy for me to get depressed, anxious, or even angry at all of the garbage in the world. There are fewer places to turn for answers, fewer people I can trust. But, in contrast to others around me who have no one to go to, I believe I can trust Jesus. That is why, as a Christian, I need to remember to see life through the filter of that belief and not let myself be emotionally swayed by the things going on around me.

A woman whose faith allows for a practical sense of hope may express herself this way:

Wife

To me, hope in Christ means that I can trust Him with the outcome, even when things look much different than what I had hoped. There are times when that is not so easy, when my fears and questions surface and I find myself on the edge of panic! But then He calmly reminds me that He has proven time and again that He will triumph.

LET ME ASK YOU THIS . . .

- Describe what it means to have "hope in Christ" in our life, family, and relationship.
- Can you think of a situation this year when you had lost a sense of hope? What were the circumstances that affected your hope in Christ? What did you learn from this experience?

A Suggested Prayer

Father, sometimes we ask, "Where are You?" We face injustice, lack of belief, and power struggles everywhere we turn. Everyone around us looks for hope, but Your Name is not called, unless it is only to defeat our enemies. We believe that hope is greater than these circumstances; it is the conviction that You are trustworthy. Please, give us more faith . . .

IDOLS

"To whom will you compare me or count me equal?
To whom will you liken me that we may be compared? Some pour
out gold from their bags and weigh out silver on the scales;
they hire a goldsmith to make it into a god, and they bow down
and worship. . . . Though one cries out to it, it does not answer;
it cannot save him from his troubles."
Isaiah 46:5-7

W e were reading from a Bible picture book. Our six-year-old wanted to know what "those yellow cows" were, and why the men were praying like that. The more I tried to explain, the deeper hole I found myself in — how do you explain to a modern child about idol worship in biblical times? How can you convince them that people actually bowed down and prayed to a golden cow? We sure couldn't do it!

Today we are far more sophisticated, and yet no less ridiculous! We don't pray to "yellow cows," now we rely on IRAs, money market funds, and the stock market to protect us from impending doom. Credit solves all of our fiscal woes. We revere modern-day mystics on TV talk shows and buy their books by the millions. We send money to "men of God" who promise us a financial return for our gifts. But at least we don't bow down to idols!

An idol is *anything that takes the place of God in your life.* It can be an image, the "security" of insurance, a job, even friends and family. For none of these can ever hope to satisfy our hunger for God. We were created in His image, and thus our lives are a never-ending search for the meaning found in knowing Him.

"Do not turn to idols or make gods of cast metal for yourselves. I am the LORD your God" (Leviticus 19:4).

Defined as anything that takes the place of God, the idea of modern-day idols may prompt a man to say this:

Husband

I haven't considered those things that give me security as idols before. It has always seemed right to be cautious and responsible with our needs and finances. In fact, I have felt like God wanted me to take care of our affairs. But I suppose there is a balance, and I step over the line far too often by relying on my skill and brains to take care of us. I wouldn't call that idol worship, but I am disturbed by the notion that there may be some things I need to change.

A woman may have different idols to deal with, and one might talk about it this way:

Wife

I confess that in my attempt to experience love and fulfillment I sometimes bypass the very Source and settle for what is instead limited but visible. I usually sacrifice my focus on the Lord for human relationships. Or I get caught up in believing that if we could only go on this trip or acquire such and such, *then* I would be happy. I *say* that nothing in life is more important to me than the Lord Jesus Christ . . . but I know I often don't really live that way.

LET ME ASK YOU THIS . . .

- When you hear the word *idol*, what comes to mind? Explain.
- What modern-day idols do you and I struggle with? What are some you yourself struggle with?

❧ How can we avoid looking to our "idols" for security and hope, and learn how to trust Jesus more?

A Suggested Prayer

Father, we confess that we have several things we often rely on for our hope and security, and we need Your mercy and forgiveness. Help us to see the idols in our lives, and give us the wisdom to conquer them . . .

INFLUENCES

"Come to me, all you who are weary and burdened, and I will give you rest. Take my yoke upon you and learn from me, for I am gentle and humble in heart, and you will find rest for your souls. For my yoke is easy and my burden is light."

Matthew 11:28-30

—————————— ♡ ——————————

All kinds of teachers seek to influence us, and not just in the classroom. Despots teach us to hate, producers teach us to watch instead of play, and advertisers teach us to need. We are not the innocent victims of these influences. We can turn off the television, cancel the subscriptions, stop going to movies, and find other teachers who will instill a different set of values. But it is easier to sit and stare, to take it all in, while fighting to deny these change agents have any power over us. But they do.

There is only One influencer we can trust. Only One who will always tell the truth, always be gentle, always be kind, and always be right. He doesn't want to sell anything to us, except a relationship, and He doesn't want to coerce or manipulate. But He has come to influence.

Jesus is the Great Teacher. He commands, but as One who has authority. He instructs, but as One who has compassion. And with so many other influences in our lives, He will seek to guide us, but He will never leave us alone. He remains with love and peace and power.

Learn from Jesus Christ. Seek His counsel, His advice. Make a choice to turn your back on those teachers who seek to destroy, and spend time learning from the One who can make you whole.

CONVERSATION STARTER

There are many who seek to influence us, and because of this some men may express their thoughts this way:

Husband

I know that I am influenced by the messengers in my life. With some I consciously make a decision not to listen; others I let have their way. I know that the methods I use to filter these messages are not totally pure, and there are many influences in life that I don't like but I still listen to them. I want more of *Jesus'* words and impact in my life, and so I must think of ways to allow Him to be my filter.

For many women, the issues may be different, as expressed here:

Wife

I constantly have to ask myself questions like these: Why do I believe what I do? What is it about my lifestyle and desires that are the products of the influences around me? How much of what I do is out of response to the expectations of others? So much comes into my life that contributes to how I think, it is a challenge to keep true to the teachings of Jesus Christ.

LET ME ASK YOU THIS . . .

- Who, or what, are some of the teachers influencing your life? How do they do it? What are some of the things they are trying to tell you?
- What are some ways Jesus could have a greater influence in your life? How could I help you experience Him more tangibly?

A Suggested Prayer

Father, there are people and messages all around us that seek to keep us from You. We confess that we have succumbed to them in more ways than we know. Save us, heal us, and teach us to walk with You; please, filter out those influences that attempt to destroy us . . .

INTEGRITY

The LORD was with Samuel as he grew up,
and he let none of his words fall to the ground.
1 Samuel 3:19

T his recent headline screamed out at me:

"91% of Americans Lie"

Johnny Carson, on *The Tonight Show,* responded: "What are they saying? Who can trust such a survey?"

The article *was* disturbing, if not surprising. Nearly everyone lies, and most have no moral problems with it.

Our cultural definition of integrity has shifted. Today morality has been reduced to one basic tenet: Don't get caught! Go ahead and lie, cheat, steal, and deceive; just be careful, or you may be found out. It seems the greatest sin is vulnerability, the greatest fear, disclosure.

Samuel was a man of integrity. He was honest. When he spoke, people could trust him. He knew that God sees the heart, and his faith was in the One who knew him and loved him anyway.

Integrity is in short supply today. A person's word used to mean something, but today it takes a receipt and a videotape to process a claim. Mistrust has infiltrated and poisoned every aspect of society. Who can we trust?

There is One who has integrity, who will never go back on His word. Jesus Christ has promised to be with us, even "to the end of the age." His character is sure, His love unshakable.

Because He is faithful and is our model for relationships, He calls us to pursue integrity. Being a person of integrity will be difficult today, but the dark world in which we live is in desperate need of the light of integrity. We need men and women who are honest, genuine, and trustworthy. The cost at times may be high—our friendships, and sometimes our jobs—but God has invited us to follow Him.

CONVERSATION STARTER

In a world where compromise is the norm, the topic of integrity may cause some men to say:

Husband

In most cases, I am basically honest. But because of the pressures in my life and the influences around me, the temptation is great to fudge every now and then. Whether it is figuring taxes, how I respond in business, or having thoughts that would make me ashamed if others knew them, I have some secret, hidden things in my life that I want to change. I see myself as a man of integrity, but there are a few areas that could use help.

A woman may see integrity in terms of her relationships, as expressed here:

Wife

Sometimes I am ashamed of the way I—as an ambassador of Jesus Christ—portray His life and character in me. Many of the times I allow myself to falter seem to be connected with a desire to "fit in" with a certain group of people. I walk away feeling disappointed in myself and wish that I was less concerned with what people think and more concerned with what my Lord feels.

LET ME ASK YOU THIS . . .

🍃 How would you define "integrity"?

🍃 Let's list some people whose lives demonstrate this quality. What about them do you think sets them apart? Do you think it is hard for them to live a life of integrity?

🍃 What are some areas where you may be inclined to compromise your integrity? Why?

🍃 Are there any "blind spots" you see in me of which I need to be aware?

A SUGGESTED PRAYER

Father, we want to be obedient to You and reveal Your light to this world. Help us to live as people who trust You enough to walk with integrity in every area of our lives . . .

JESUS' BIRTH

In the beginning was the Word, and the Word was with God,
and the Word was God. . . . The Word became flesh
and made his dwelling among us.

John 1:1,14

— ♡ —

The invasion that shook the world! Hinted at for centuries, when the day finally arrived, few were aware that He had come—a few shepherds, some distant relatives, and a handful of travelers from the East. There was no fanfare, no royal announcement, no welcome for the King. His humble entry into our world went largely unnoticed . . . at the time.

But His presence has been felt ever since. When God became a man He ushered in a whole new era. No longer was He a God whose majesty and power made Him always seem bigger than life; no longer to be awed and admired only at arm's length—He became, and continues to be, a Person to be known. He feels, He shouts, He kisses, and He weeps! Jesus Christ is the visible, tangible, touchable expression of the invisible God.

Has He entered your world? How did He come? Is He silently and slowly making His presence felt, or is He clearly reigning as King? His birth in the stable at Bethlehem was a prelude to His invitation to be born in our lives. Has He been born in you?

CONVERSATION STARTER

Depending on background and history, some men may

express their thoughts about the birth of Jesus in the following way:

Husband
Christmas means a great deal to me. I love the season, but also I am excited because of the birth of Jesus. It is exciting to know that He wants to be born in me, as opposed to being a God who resides somewhere "out there." I hear it all the time; I know it is true. Yet, when it *really* sinks in, I find it both comforting and scary. When God's Spirit comes to dwell in me, He is so close to me that I can never hide from Him or flee His presence.

Women may have these thoughts about Jesus' coming to earth:

Wife
It is hard for me to remember that the God of this universe has an emotional side much like ours. I tend to think of Him as so totally in control that *He* doesn't *get* hurt. I find that I must regularly seek His forgiveness for not considering His feelings and how it must affect Him when I disregard or disobey Him. He is very real in my life, but I need to remember His name—Immanuel, God with us.

LET ME ASK YOU THIS . . .
- What does the birth of Jesus mean to you?
- How does His birth affect your life each day?
- What comes to mind when you realize that Christ's Spirit is actually alive in you? Let's talk about the implications of these things.

A SUGGESTED PRAYER
Lord Jesus, thank You for entering our world. Thank You that Your humble beginnings brought to us the gift of intimacy and friendship with You. Be born in us today . . .

JESUS' DEATH

God demonstrates his own love for us in this:
While we were still sinners, Christ died for us.
Romans 5:8

A s darkness grew over that foul place called Skull
Hill, a foreboding air settled in. On the hill itself
nothing seemed particularly out of the ordinary,
for the Romans had killed hundreds on Golgatha. But
the prisoner, He was no ordinary criminal; this man was
different. A few days ago the crowds had been singing
His praises; now they wanted His blood. But there was
something about Him that caused even the most seasoned
of executioners to take pause.

God remained determined; no level of cruelty could
stop Jesus. The illegal trial, the endless questions, the
mocking from the temple guards, and the beatings by
the Romans could not daunt Him. "Like a lamb to the
slaughter . . . he did not open his mouth," Isaiah foretold
this day 600 years before (Isaiah 53:7). How could they
do it—beat, torture, and mock the One who had created
them?

But Jesus wasn't to be stopped. There were precious
loved ones to be rescued, and His love demanded that He
die. So, on that bitter, lonely hill, Jesus cried out, "It is
finished!" And He died.

Preachers call it the Passion of Christ, and the emotions it evokes in men and women cannot be described.

But He does not want our pity, nor even a distant expression of gratitude. He wants *us*. He died to free us from the chains of self and to give us life with Him.

CONVERSATION STARTER
Christ's sacrifice on the cross evokes different emotions in each person, and a couple may respond like this:

Husband
I often get angry over the cruelty of that day. But then there are times when I can see how I could have done the same thing to Jesus, had I been there. And that brings home for me the power of what Jesus did on the cross — I am deeply guilty, and yet, He died anyway. I can't fathom Jesus' love for me, but I deeply, deeply appreciate it.

Wife
Rarely can I hear the story of the crucifixion without being moved to tears and deeply hurt by the pain my Lord endured for me. My sorrow is that on a day-to-day basis I do not always live with the same sensitivity in my heart toward Him.

LET ME ASK YOU THIS . . .
&. What are some of the elements of Christ's crucifixion that strike you the most? Why?
&. When was the first time you consciously remember hearing about Jesus' death? Do you remember your response?
&. In talking about the cross, what thoughts go through your mind even now?

A SUGGESTED PRAYER
Lord God, we are overwhelmed by the meaning of the cross, by how much You love us, and how much it cost You. To say thank You is not enough, for Your love demands a response . . .

JESUS' RESURRECTION

If it is preached that Christ has been raised from the dead,
how can some of you say that there is no resurrection of the dead?

1 Corinthians 15:12

The rock upon which the Christian experience is built is the resurrection of Jesus Christ. The sheer evidence is so compelling, many have come to know Him *while attempting to destroy the faith*. The rallying cry of the saints, "He is alive!" brings hope to the world.

While many sing boldly "Christ the Lord is risen today," how deeply does the reality of the risen Christ penetrate? He is alive at our work, but do we recognize Him? He lives with our friends, but how often do we mention Him? He lives in our homes, but where is He included?

Jesus' resurrection also brings His presence to the very heart of our marriage. He comes with compassion, understanding, healing, peace, wisdom, and power. But is He embraced? Do we invite Him to join us as we eat, sleep, talk, fight, and enjoy sex? Or is His presence a theological afterthought remembered in times of crisis?

Let your life sing out, "Christ the Lord is risen today, alleluia!"

CONVERSATION STARTER

The implications of Christ's resurrection are limitless, and many couples may express their thoughts like this:

Husband

When I think about it, I know that Jesus is alive and active in the world today. If I would only take some time to dwell on that one truth, my outlook on life, my relationships, and my schedule would change dramatically. I do believe that He is in my office, my home, and my bedroom, but it has yet to be very real to me. Perhaps the problem is that I have so few people I can talk to about Christ. There must be one or two who would understand.

Wife

The cares of this world often block my vision, making it difficult for me to see Jesus in the routine of the every day. I get so consumed with my to-do lists and those little emergencies that seem to overwhelm my schedule, I can run for hours without a thought about Jesus. My prayer is that Jesus would teach me to see Him in my tasks and relationships.

LET ME ASK YOU THIS . . .

- ﹥ Are there any areas of your life in which you regularly experience the reality of the risen Christ? Describe them.
- ﹥ In what area of your life do you find it difficult to see Jesus? Why?
- ﹥ What are some areas where you rarely (if ever) experience Jesus as the risen Savior? How can you acknowledge Him in a more tangible way in one or two of these areas?

A SUGGESTED PRAYER

Lord Jesus, as we pray we want to experience the reality of Your resurrection. Help us to see You more clearly in every area of our lives. Help us to experience You in our relationship, as we seek to invite You in . . .

JOY

Rejoice in the Lord always.
I will say it again: Rejoice!
Philippians 4:4

As our two-year-old sat in the car singing, "I've got that joy, joy, joy, joy down in my heart," I was forced to ask myself, "Do *I* have that joy?"

Everyone wants to be able to follow the Apostle Paul's advice and "Rejoice in the Lord always." In this day of catchy slogans, these words can have an empty sound to them. It *sounds* good to rejoice always, but it is much easier said than done. With just the right amount of money and planning, there are some who find a degree of happiness. But the kind of joy Paul speaks of comes from a far deeper place. Who among us *wouldn't* want to rejoice always if we could just figure out how? If only our hearts were tuned to God.

It is interesting that shortly after Paul wrote the words of Philippians 4:4, he also wrote, "I have learned the secret of being content in any and every situation, whether well fed or hungry, whether living in plenty or in want" (verse 12). A secret producing that kind of joy regardless of circumstances would be the news of the century! How can I get hold of this secret?

"I can do everything through him who gives me strength" (verse 13). The secret is this: *The closer my connection to the One who brings life, the deeper my contentment, and thus the greater my joy.* It has nothing to do with money, or status, or performance. It is knowing that I matter.

People value finding happiness over everything else today, and yet — if they would open their eyes — they would find it right in front of them. Beware the temptation to produce joy by *what you do,* for it will never work. Joy is found only in an alive relationship with Jesus Christ and His body of believers.

CONVERSATION STARTER

In seeking after joy, some men may say this:

Husband
Many things make me happy, but joy is something that is a bit more elusive. To be like Paul, completely content in any circumstance and able to know joy wherever I am, attracts me. I really want to find ways to deepen my relationship with Jesus.

Some women may talk about their struggles to remain joyful in this way:

Wife
Those times when I am closest to the Lord, I feel an incredible joy that I know is not of this world. The difficult thing for me is to continue living that joy when the circumstances of life are tough. The more life begins to press in on me, the harder it is for me to feel close to Jesus and, therefore, to rediscover the joy He has for me.

LET ME ASK YOU THIS . . .
- What is your definition of joy?
- Do you believe it is possible to rejoice *always* as Paul challenges us to do? What would it mean in everyday life?
- If you can rejoice always, what secret has the Lord offered to help you get there? If you can't, why not?

A Suggested Prayer

Father, thank You for the promise of joy to those who walk with You. Thank You for the joy we have in knowing You. Help us to recognize that joy each day . . .

LONELINESS

How long, O LORD? Will you forget me forever? How long will you hide your face from me? How long must I wrestle with my thoughts and every day have sorrow in my heart?

Psalm 13:1-2

"The loneliest people I've ever met are in the business world," a friend recently remarked.

"I don't agree," another replied. "The loneliest people I have met are women who stay home with their kids."

How do you judge such a thing? And why bother? Loneliness is all around us, and it knows no boundaries. There are lonely bankers, lonely waitresses, and lonely politicians. It makes little difference if they are surrounded by others or not, for *loneliness is a matter of the heart.*

Loneliness is similar to a stream created during a rainstorm. The longer the storm, the greater the deluge. As the storm clears, the creek dries in the warmth of the sun.

Our own storm may begin with a painful relationship, a poor performance, or a busy schedule filled with tasks that keeps us from interacting with others. Like the water, loneliness starts to move slowly, but if fed and encouraged, it soon becomes a torrent of pain.

David's cry in Psalm 13 was a floodgate of emotion. He cried out to God for deliverance as he was in the midst of his sorrow. But David knew the antidote to the despair he was feeling—"I will sing to the LORD, for he has been good to me" (verse 6).

The same is true for you and me when we struggle with the pain of loneliness. We must sing to the Lord, even when we don't *feel* like singing. Tell God that we trust Him, even as we wallow in the pit. For, despite all the feelings of the moment, *He has been good to us!*

CONVERSATION STARTER

Loneliness may be epidemic, but we seldom discuss it. In light of this silence, some couples may express their feelings like this:

Husband

A frightening sense of loneliness inside me occasionally rears its ugly head. I try to push it out of my mind, and usually I can use my business as a shield to keep from thinking about it. But in the long run, there is no escaping my struggle deep inside with being lonely. When I *do* admit my pain to the Lord and a few friends, I feel better. Even though I am afraid to face my loneliness, it is good to know that Jesus provides an alternative.

Wife

Even in the midst of a busy, rich life I sometimes feel lonely and wonder if anyone in this world can relate to the feelings within my heart. I know there are many who *do* care and *want* to be there for me, but during the times when I am lonely, I am blind to their love for me. Often when I feel this way, the Lord uses some person or circumstance to remind me of His constant tenderness toward me, and I am able to move on.

LET ME ASK YOU THIS . . .

ꙮ How do you identify with this idea of loneliness? Do you ever experience feelings of loneliness? Is there a particular set of circumstances that can lead you there?

🙢 When you are lonely, do you tend to shy away from others in your loneliness or seek me out, or a friend, to comfort you? Why do you respond that way?

🙢 What help has the Lord offered you during times of loneliness? How can I help?

A Suggested Prayer

Father, we ask You to comfort those who are experiencing the sorrow of loneliness right now. Help us to be Your compassionate answer to their cries. Remind us, too, Father, of Your love for us when we are lonely . . .

LYING

Do not lie to each other, since you have taken off your old self
with its practices and have put on the new self,
which is being renewed in knowledge in the image of its Creator.

Colossians 3:9-10

"I'll just keep this to myself; it's better that way."
The white lie—what can it hurt?
When we allow that first single act of deceit, the seed of distrust begins to have a chance to take root. As soon as we compromise our relationship, for whatever reason, it becomes easier the second time, and the next, and the next. The deception begins with a small lie that seems to cause no harm. Then, it leads to a negative comment, a hidden purchase, wandering eyes, a secret alliance. From the most trivial of infractions can grow a cancer that can kill a relationship.

The greatest danger lies in the hiding. No marriage is immune from misunderstanding and selfishness. When we *know* we have broken the trust of our partner, we must confess our transgression, ask for forgiveness, and be willing to change. Cleansing and health are products of reconciliation. But whenever we try to hide, we are finished.

As the highest commitment in human relationships, marriage requires trust to maintain its bond. To lie is to violate trust.

As we live out our love for Christ and one another, "Do not lie to each other."

Some men say that it is impossible to survive in business without lying. Within that environment, then, many men may feel like this:

Husband

I know it is wrong to lie, especially to my wife. But I do it anyway, sometimes. Not lying really, but I do have those times when I reveal somewhat less than the truth. When found out, I sheepishly grin and admit to the infraction. I say to myself for the hundredth time, "You fool, why do you have to lie? You *love* her!" I want her to trust me, and so I feel bad on those occasions when I deceive her.

Lying can so easily be explained away as a game between a couple that a woman may feel this way:

Wife

I tend to justify my little white lies. I assume that it is best for the relationship if I don't bring something up, in order to avoid a fight. When I play that game too often, however, I feel myself getting further and further away from my husband. I don't like the feeling of dishonesty that creeps in and separates us.

LET ME ASK YOU THIS . . .

- Honestly, now, has there been a time lately when you were less than truthful with me over anything? If so, can you describe what caused you to feel the need to do that?
- Do you believe there are any circumstances (other than birthday surprises and the like) where it is right to intentionally hide something from each other, or even outright lie?
- From your experience, how have hidden secrets affected our relationship, or your other relationships?

A SUGGESTED PRAYER

Father, bring us closer together right now. Help us to forgive each other for the subtle ways we hurt each other,
and help us to be completely honest in all we say and
do. Move us to want to change, to grow; and give us the
wisdom and resources to come together as a couple committed to truth in our marriage . . .

MENTORS

As for you, continue in what you have learned and have become
convinced of, because you know those from whom you learned it.

2 Timothy 3:14

T wo people of the same age and background wanted to go into the ministry.

The biggest difference was that one sought advice, counsel, and friendship with others and the other wanted more to be admired than to be known. One went on to touch a great many lives with her sensitivity and humble nature, and the other's brash manner and arrogant style forced him out of every organization that hired him.

This scenario is common, even in the church. Those who keep others at arm's length tend to want to "go it alone." They tend to become hardened and narrow. Yet those who welcome accountable relationships will develop the compassion and sensitivity to make an impact on the lives of others.

This type of growth comes only through relation-ships. We all need a mentor—someone who can teach us, guide us, and hold us accountable. Few take the time to find someone whom they respect and trust with their life. But, if we, like Timothy, look for the Paul whom God has for us, and watch them carefully, seeking their advice and input, our lives may be used to change the world.

CONVERSATION STARTER

As a result of growing up in an individualist society, few men and women have sought out accountable relationships, especially in a mentor-like role. Some couples may talk about this type of relationship like this:

Husband

The closest thing I have had to a mentor is a friend I see now and then whom I respect. His life is an example to me, and I always feel that I receive something from him when we talk. But, have I ever met on a regular basis with a mentor? No, I haven't known anyone who would do that with me. Even if I did, I wouldn't know where to begin.

Wife

I think that I would really benefit from the presence of an older, wiser woman in my life. Someone I respect, who is a little further down the road than I am. But, even if I were able to find that type of woman, I would feel silly approaching her and not know what to say. Perhaps the reason I haven't looked for the right person is because I've been waiting for God to drop her in my lap.

LET ME ASK YOU THIS . . .

- Describe your idea of a "mentor." Have you ever had one? If so, what was your relationship like? If not, how do you feel about that?
- Have you ever been a mentor to someone else? If so, describe your relationship. If not, why not?
- If you desire a mentor in your life now, who comes to mind that you would respect and enjoy? Are there any reasons why you wouldn't want to ask that person to fulfill that role for a while?
- If you want to be a mentor to someone else, does anyone come to mind? What are some reasons that you would be a good mentor for that person?

A Suggested Prayer

Father, thank You for the times we learn from each other. Thank You that there are people around us who would care for us and help us to grow, if we investigate the possibilities. Help each of us to seek out someone who could be a mentor, and bring someone to mind whom we could begin mentoring . . .

MONEY

Keep your lives free from the love of money
and be content with what you have,
because God has said, "Never will I leave you;
never will I forsake you."

Hebrews 13:5

T he Lord never said that money is evil. It is a neutral
resource necessary in an ordered society. It has great
potential for good; money used wisely can comfort
the disadvantaged, house the homeless, feed the hungry,
tangibly care for the broken and the friendless. It can provide the means for bringing the good news of Jesus Christ
to those who otherwise might not hear. Without it we cannot meet even the basic necessities of life.

Look again at these words: "Keep your lives free from
the love of money." It is not just the money that we love,
but what money can do for us. Money bestows power—to
control others, to never need, to never want. When we
love money we can deceive ourselves into thinking we
are smarter, kinder, and more healthy than we are. The
love of money manipulates, distorts, and enraptures. If we
believe that money can bring joy, satisfaction, and peace
to our lives, we have lost control over the resource and
have succumbed to its seduction.

God's injunction to keep "free from the love of money"
is tied to His promise to remain with us through any
circumstances. He will never let us down. It is not money
that will sustain us. The Lord knows what we need—we
need *Him.*

CONVERSATION STARTER

Everyone has strong opinions when it comes to money. For men, a common reaction to the subject may be:

Husband

I wish I had more money. Imagine the good I could do with it if I had more. But, on the other hand, I would probably want even more. I want to be a giving person, and yet I am afraid of losing control of our finances. Sometimes I am generous, but then I wake up to the realization that my generosity has strings attached, so I give, but not enough.

For women, money can be a difficult issue, and there are few things that affect a marriage like it. Perhaps they would express their feelings like this:

Wife

Money is one of the toughest issues in our marriage. When I am not working outside of the home and contributing to the budget, it is difficult for me to feel like an equal, or that I have any control over our finances. Consequently, I often feel powerless and that I have to account to my husband for what I spend. I don't like that feeling at all.

LET ME ASK YOU THIS . . .

- Are you comfortable with the way our budget and finances are set up right now? If not, why not? If we need to, how could we change things?
- In what ways does money bring joy to our lives? Peace? Security? Does this stand in the way of trusting Jesus for these things?
- How much money do we give away each month? Is it enough? In what ways should we consider expanding our giving?

A Suggested Prayer

Father, we confess that money often keeps us from relying completely on You. We recognize that our hope, our lives, our security must be in You if we want to know what it means to live in relationship with You. In this confusing world, we often look to the power money brings to meet these needs. Free us from the love of money, and develop in us the desire to give as You have given to us . . .

MOODS

When my heart was grieved and my spirit embittered,
I was senseless and ignorant; I was a brute beast before you.
Yet I am always with you; you hold me by my right hand.

Psalm 73:21-23

Having been from Los Angeles, living in Colorado took some getting used to. The people are great, and the mountains are beautiful, but the weather took us by surprise. There's a saying here: "If you don't like the weather, wait ten minutes"! Even now, as the "experts" predicted a fine spring day with highs in the sixties, the snow gently piles on our newly planted tulips.

Moods are like that. Unpredictable and uncontrollable, they invade our lives without warning. They affect us all in different ways, but no one is immune from their power. A bad day at work, a cold coming on, or a sudden attack of the "blues" can put the most placid into a tailspin. Too often we take it out on those we are closest to.

Who doesn't have those days when, for one reason or another, we are cranky, or sullen, or melancholy? When they hit, it may feel as if no one understands. The fights loom larger, and the conflicts more potent, yet our need to be loved and understood for what we are feeling is all the more keen.

Therein lies an important gift of the Scriptures, and the psalms in particular. We are invited to come and openly lay ourselves before the throne of Heaven *as we are*, not as we are *expected* to be. There is no pretense with God—He knows us anyway, so we may as well be honest with Him. He will never ask us to hide who we are or what we feel. He asks us to come before Him and joyfully acknowledge that He is the Lord who is worthy of our trust and honesty.

We may fear that even God would withdraw in the midst of our moods, but the Father can never be turned off by our moods. As the psalmist said, "Yet I am always with you; you hold me by my right hand."

CONVERSATION STARTER

As much as we would like to be consistent, we all have those days when we are less than perfect, which may be summarized:

Husband

It may be because of the weather, a slight cold, or being overly tired, but when I am sullen I need my wife, my kids, and my coworkers to just let me be. It is eye-opening for me to realize that God does just that, and I can come to Him even in the worst of moods. That type of acceptance is the quickest antidote to help me snap out of the blues.

Wife

When I am in a bad mood there is usually something deeper that I am not even aware of. During those times, I need to be accepted for who I am without having to explain myself. Sometimes, by saying I am in a bad mood, I rationalize my crabbiness, thus giving no one permission to question my actions. I want the freedom to be myself, and yet I don't want to blindly hurt others or be a prisoner of my feelings.

LET ME ASK YOU THIS . . .

- ❧ How do I act when I am in a bad mood? How do you feel about this?
- ❧ Do you believe that I give you permission to keep

me in check while in a bad mood, or do I keep you at arm's length?

- Are you ever frightened or hurt by my bad moods? If you can, give me some specific examples.
- How can God help you in the midst of your bad moods?

A SUGGESTED PRAYER

Father, thank You for loving us right where we are, in our present stage of growth. Thank You for Your patience and forgiveness, and for Your desire to be with us even when our hearts are cold and our attitudes less than loving. In those times of emotional darkness, give us the sensitivity to be careful with those around us and the wisdom to come to You — warts and all . . .

PAIN

He [Jesus] said to her, "Daughter, your faith has healed you.
Go in peace and be freed from your suffering."
Mark 5:34

Over lunch recently, a friend told me about his wife's daily struggle with cancer. She has defeated the odds by staying alive this long, and she courageously hangs on despite the pain and sorrow.

God's name came up in the conversation. "Where is He? Why doesn't He intervene? Is He angry with us, or worse, has He abandoned us?" All I could do was listen to my friend and weep with him. We discussed God's faithfulness and mercy, but those difficult questions lingered unanswered.

To live is to feel pain: for in a broken world, struggle is the norm. We want it to be different. We want our commitment to faith to make us deserving of a life of comfort and safety. Somehow God must penetrate and heal, just as He did on that dusty road for the bleeding woman (Mark 5:24-34). But even a casual look at Jesus' ministry compels us to face this truth: Life on earth is filled with heartache, disease, loneliness, and pain.

A greater truth can be discovered in the midst of the struggle. *Jesus understands.* He walked the streets of Jerusalem bearing the instrument of His death, hearing the insults and laughter, bleeding from the wounds of insensitivity and corrupted power. He hung under the darkened sky, experiencing the anguish of separation from His Father. By His suffering, Jesus has silenced the critics who continue to lash out at Him, "You just don't understand!"

CONVERSATION STARTER

Pain is not a favorite subject of men, and some may express their thoughts this way:

Husband

The busier I am, the more I am able to ignore the fact that we live in a world filled with pain and sorrow. I do not like to acknowledge that I must expect pain, and so I do my best not to think about it. My insulation has kept me artificially secure — just enough to be impotent to help those who are deep in pain. Only when I face the reality that pain is all around me will I be able to be a friend to those who need me. But I have a long way to go.

Although women are sometimes more willing to acknowledge the reality of pain and bring comfort to others, they still struggle, as expressed in this comment:

Wife

Pain makes me uncomfortable in that it takes away my ability to be in control. I would much rather deny its existence than allow it to affect my life. But when someone I love is in pain and needs me, I cannot ignore it. I must be there to share in his or her struggle.

LET ME ASK YOU THIS . . .

- Describe the most painful experience you had as a child. What were the circumstances? Who comforted you?
- How did (do) your parents respond to pain? Who was (is) better at facing pain directly in times of crisis, your mom or dad? As a child, were you able to talk about pain with your parents?

🙶 Who in your life is in the most pain right now? How can you bring the love and comfort of Christ to that person?

A SUGGESTED PRAYER

Father God, Scripture calls You "the Father of compassion and the God of all comfort" (2 Corinthians 1:3). Please bring Your love and healing power to those who are in pain right now. Thank You for the costly gift You gave us through the cross and the suffering Your Son experienced to let us know how much You identify with our pain. Give us the wisdom to care for those who are in pain, to seek Your peace, and to be Your instrument to reach out to them . . .

PARENTS

*Listen, my son, to your father's instruction and do not forsake
your mother's teaching. They will be a garland
to grace your head and a chain to adorn your neck.*

Proverbs 1:8-9

We never come alone to marriage. Who we are is
a complex mix of multiple influences and per-
sonalities. Yes, we are individuals in our character by God's creation, but our parents (and others) have
made an indelible mark on our lives.

As our marriage grows, there seem to be more pressing things we need to tackle—finances, pride, careers,
children. But one issue remains the "wild card": our
parents.

For some of us, the history we bear is painfully
unhealthy—codependence, criticism, debasement, abuse.
Then there are those who bring a rich family tradition of
friendship and stability to their marriage. But for most,
the memories of our parents are a mixed bag—pain, joy,
tenderness, rejection, fun, disappointment. Even with the
best of parents, almost every child vows never to be like
them. As adults, we may love our parents, and even like
them, but most of us still feel like adolescents trying to
prove ourselves and go our own way.

Every family is different, and every relationship
unique. Do you need to step back and consider your
parents' past influence and current involvement? Could
unresolved pain be keeping you from heeding the words

from Proverbs? Or are you able to love your parents as God's gift to the adult you?

When it comes to family, many men emotionally left home long ago. But in light of the mark parents make, a man may say this:

Husband
I like to think that I am a man who is basically free from my parents' influence over me. But as my own kids grow, I see more characteristics of my dad and mom in me. My usual response is, "They are a part of my past. That was then, this is now." But in my heart I know that's not true. The fact is I don't really know how to relate to my parents, and they don't know how to relate to me.

Although women are gone from their parents' home physically, the ties to family may remain strong, as expressed here:

Wife
The older I get and the more of life I experience the greater my appreciation for my parents. As a parent, I can see the sacrifices my parents made for me, and are still making, because I am their child. They continue to give and give, even as I have matured and moved away from them. The question for me now is this: How do I be my own person, the individual God wants *me* to be, separate from them?

LET ME ASK YOU THIS . . .
- On a scale of 1 to 10 (10 representing the closest) how do you rate your relationship with your parents? What about your relationship with my parents? Why did you choose those numbers?
- In what ways do you think I carry positive influences of my parents into our relationship? Negative influences?

❧ How can we help each other deepen our relationships with our parents?

A SUGGESTED PRAYER

Father God, thank You for the gift of my parents. We confess that we are often critical and think more of ourselves than of their needs. Forgive us. Help us to seek to love and understand them more. Give us a deeper sense of appreciation for what they have done . . .

PEACE

"Peace I leave with you; my peace I give you.
I do not give you as the world gives.
Do not let your hearts be troubled and do not be afraid."
John 14:27

A warm August night . . . a mountain top . . . a symphony . . . children playing . . . a snow-covered valley.

Within the depths of the imagination, every person has their own private picture of peace. Unique in expression, but universal in meaning—it is filled with contentment, beauty, and rest.

Some people claim to have mastered the ability to encounter heavenly peace at a moment's notice, even in the midst of a hectic schedule. But few can do that. Our hearts are filled with fear and worry, keeping peace from having its way. Most people believe that to realize peace they must get away. We need time to shed the anxiety of the moment before we can inhale the peaceful fragrance of God.

But the peace of Christ is more than a feeling, mood, or sense of quiet contentment and focus. The peace of Christ is an inner sense that, because we know Him, all is well. We may be flustered and troubled on the surface, but the promise of Christ is that His peace will ultimately reign.

Seek Him in the quiet moments, acknowledge Him in the midst of the storm, and His peace will cover you.

CONVERSATION STARTER

In a world filled with strife and struggle, peace is a rare commodity. One couple may express their understanding of peace like this:

Husband

I suppose when I think about it, my faith does offer me a sense of calm in the midst of a crazy and hectic life. I almost never, however, experience the kind of gentle peace that I've heard others describe. Sometimes, if I get up early enough, I get a glimpse of it and find it very reassuring, powerful. But all too quickly I get distracted by the urgency of my day. I desire that peace, though, and want to learn how to discover it for myself.

Wife

I know that Jesus Christ offers a peace not of this world, a peace that is unshakable. I've experienced it! The hard part for me is to get in a position away from the unrest of daily life where I am able to *receive* Him and the gifts He has for me. I confess that I need help to hear His voice.

LET ME ASK YOU THIS . . .

- Do you sense a general inner peace because of your faith? If so, describe it. If not, does this disturb you?
- How can we as a couple experience the quiet peace of Christ? How can we do that as individuals? Can we help each other?

A SUGGESTED PRAYER

Father, we want the peace You have for us. We confess that we *do* let our hearts be troubled and we are sometimes anxious and fearful. Give us the wisdom to trust You to be able to find and lean on Your peace . . .

PERFORMANCE

Now the Lord is the Spirit,
and where the Spirit of the Lord is, there is freedom.
2 Corinthians 3:17

An observer might summarize our culture this way: "Achievement is the foundation upon which happiness, health, and prosperity rest. Nothing else really matters."

For men, our heroes are the stars, those success stories who have built financial empires from management disasters. Or the athletes who keep our weary minds occupied from week to week, so we don't have to consider how little of life we experience ourselves.

A woman, on the other hand, may compare herself to the neighborhood celebrity whose house is newer, bigger, and cleaner, whose children are well-dressed, charming, and spotless. This primadonna gives you that knowing smile, because she knows *you know* how incredible she is. Her husband adores her, she is never tired, and all of her friends are just like her!

How tragic when we use such worldly models as our standard of performance. As God walks steadily beside us, gently calling our names in the attempt to get our attention, He weeps over the comparison and our inability to see into people's hearts. The hero? He's frightened you may discover how anxious he is that his world may crumble. The starlet? Behind her mask she hides a lonely despair that only alcohol seems to ease. And Jesus? He has come to give freedom and life to those who reject pretense and are willing to drop to their knees in humble adoration of the One who died for them. And He keeps walking beside each of us, waiting for just the right moment to call us back to sanity.

CONVERSATION STARTER

Given the state of our culture today, with its competition in business and busy calendars, many men may feel this way about the issue of performance:

Husband

If I don't perform well, regardless of the arena (whether it's business, church, sports, or as a dad), it affects me. Sometimes I feel that my life is nothing but a string of "have to's" and "shoulds." I *know* I am loved by God as I am, but if I *really* believe that, then why is it so important for me to perform well? Even when I think about God's love, it is hard to keep my own performance standards in perspective.

Whether women choose to be full-time homemakers or to be employed outside the home, they often face a different struggle than their husbands. They may talk about their feelings like this:

Wife

For me it is not how I perform a task that matters most, but how others view me as a person. The roles I play—especially as a wife, mother, and friend—are where I am most vulnerable. I resent the pressure I sometimes feel to be someone other than who God made me to be. But because of my need for the approval of others, I struggle daily with living up to their expectations.

LET ME ASK YOU THIS . . .

🙾 List three areas where you feel the need to perform.

- Is there anything I can do to help you be free from the need to perform?
- Do you ever feel the need to perform for me? What am I doing that causes you to feel that way?

A Suggested Prayer

Father God, help us to be so convinced of Your love for us that we seek only Your approval in our day-to-day pilgrimage. We confess that we have allowed others' expectations, even those of our spouse, to mold us. We need Your help, Father, to be free from the need to perform, and to live aware of Your grace . . .

PRAYER

O God, you are my God, earnestly I seek you;
my soul thirsts for you, my body longs for you,
in a dry and weary land where there is no water.

Psalm 63:1

Our son Robbie prays about *everything!* Whether it is a problem with a friend, a sore knee, a soccer game, or a Nintendo challenge, he bows his head and calls to action the character of God. Were you to ask him if God hears his prayers, or if Jesus honestly cares about his needs, he would look at you as if you had lost your marbles!

Robbie *knows* that God hears him and that He loves him enough to answer. Sometimes yes, sometimes no, but He always answers. To Robbie, Jesus is his friend—and friends talk, don't they?

There are many reasons people don't pray. Some feel that prayer is difficult, that it takes a lot of time and effort. Others aren't sure whether God actually hears them, or that He cares enough to answer, or that "He already has determined His will, so what's the use?" So prayers go unsaid.

But prayer is easy when we see God clearly through eyes like Robbie's. Prayer is not coming into His presence; it is recognizing that He is already there, wanting nothing more than to be quietly with us. Prayer is God's way of bringing us into relationship with Him. As we come before Him in childlike faith and seek His power and wisdom, He will answer. It is then that we are made whole.

The Apostle Paul instructs us, "Pray continually" (1 Thessalonians 5:17).

CONVERSATION STARTER

Though they know about the value of prayer, many men may still express their thoughts this way:

Husband

There have been times in my life when I prayed regularly, or tried to. Over the years I find, when I do consider praying, I don't give it high priority in my life. Maybe the biggest reason I don't pray as often as I should is because I must not think it makes much difference. I know better, and I *believe* in seeking God through prayer, but I'm not often challenged about my lack of faith.

Although the role a woman plays in each situation may be different, some wives may feel like this:

Wife

Since I have three young children, my prayer life has been forced to change. As hard as I have tried to find those moments of quietness in my day, there *always* seem to be interruptions of some kind. The Lord has been teaching me more about prayer as an *attitude of the heart*, in addition to prayer as a discipline.

LET ME ASK YOU THIS . . .

- How do you define prayer?
- What role has prayer played in your relationship with God and faith in Jesus Christ?
- Describe your prayer life—frequency, depth, structure, and so on. How do you think this can become a more impacting and rich experience?
- What is one thing I could pray for you right now?

A SUGGESTED PRAYER

Father, thank You for standing by us and hearing us when we pray. We confess that at times we have lost confidence in Your character. Forgive us. Help us to not forget Your promise to hear our prayers and to meet our every need . . .

PRESSING ON

Not that I have already attained all this, or have already been made
perfect, but I press on to take hold of that for which Christ Jesus
took hold of me. Brothers, I do not consider myself yet to have
taken hold of it. But one thing I do: Forgetting what is behind and
straining toward what is ahead, I press on toward the goal to win
the prize for which God has called me heavenward in Christ Jesus.

Philippians 3:12-14

T he biggest difference between five-year-olds playing basketball and professionals is the level of intensity. Pros care if they win; small children are happy
to have a T-shirt and a post-game snack.

To press on is to care whether or not I win. I value the
game and the outcome, and I am determined to finish the
course to the best of my ability. Every professional knows
this to be true. Whether it is a professional parent, teacher,
salesperson, or doctor, the professional will sacrifice with
the necessary intensity it takes to win.

When we profess faith in Christ, in even a greater
way we are called to press on. For in life, there is no
greater goal than to finish the race of faith, to honor
our heavenly Father, and to win the prize of salvation.
Be careful of the tendency to think the race is won, or
that God is not concerned with how we live. The Bible
constantly challenges us to strive to the end in our devotion to Christ, with the goal of being invited home to be
with Him.

CONVERSATION STARTER

In light of the pressures of today's fast-paced world, a
husband and wife may express themselves like this:

Husband

It is easy for me to be focused on what I believe is important—and my faith is important. But it is also easy to lose perspective, and place other priorities ahead of my desire to follow Christ with all my heart. When I do, I need a gentle nudge to remind me of what is really important.

Wife

It is sometimes easy for me to become apathetic in my relationship with Christ. I get caught up in my family, friends, and busy lifestyle, and before I know it I've overlooked Jesus and my heart has become paralyzed, my spirit lazy. In the depths of my heart I want to be *totally* His and "run the race" with all I have, yet admittedly, I often fall short.

LET ME ASK YOU THIS . . .

- How do you feel about the idea of "pressing on"? Guilty? Motivated? Encouraged? Why do you feel that way?
- As followers of Christ, what are we supposed to strive for?
- Do you feel that the Lord is pleased with your level of endurance at this point in the race?
- What does it mean for you to give your very best?

A SUGGESTED PRAYER

Father, we confess that we are often complacent with our faith. We allow the pressure of immediate circumstances to crowd out our need to "press on" with You. Through Your Spirit, help us to do our best as we focus on the goal . . .

REST

"Remember the Sabbath day by keeping it holy. . . .
For in six days the LORD made the heavens and the earth, the sea,
and all that is in them, but he rested on the seventh day."
Exodus 20:8,11

P erhaps the greatest plague of modern culture is busyness. There is much to be said for honest toil and labor, but our full schedules often go far beyond the normal work patterns of everyday living. We are consumed with activity. More tired on Monday than on Friday, most of us have forgotten how to rest.

Perhaps the issue is related to fear—a fear subtly whispering that to slow down would be devastating. Slowing down would cause me to reflect, to be still, and to listen. I might realize how lonely I really am. It is much easier to keep the television on, allow the phone to ring off the hook, run errand after errand, if only to fill the time.

The greatest gift of the Sabbath was the permission God gave to enjoy the life He bestowed. To worship Him, to be with family and friends, to sit and talk and think and sing and pray were the purposes of the Sabbath. The Lord knows that rest is a necessary element of the life He has for us.

Too bad, really, that most Christian traditions have left behind the intent of the Sabbath. In our effort to honor Christ on the "Lord's day," we have filled our days, leaving no room for rest. On the other hand, Jesus gave merit, I suppose, to doing good on the Sabbath. When else would you play golf, mow the lawn, do the shopping, watch the games . . . ?

CONVERSATION STARTER

In regard to the topic of rest, some men may express their views like this:

Husband

I love to rest, but I don't often have that luxury. Whenever I plan on spending a quiet day at home with my family, there seems to always be another project or obligation staring me in the face. Sometimes I long for the days when families would stay home once a week and enjoy each other, and then other times I want to be left alone to sleep on the couch!

A woman may have a completely different view on the need to rest, as expressed here:

Wife

I think I have to be out of town in order to really "let down" and rest. Otherwise I find a million projects around the house to do, or places and people we need to see. The only time I can really sit down is when I have something constructive to do while I'm sitting.

LET ME ASK YOU THIS . . .

- ❧ Do you believe it is necessary to rest?
- ❧ How good are you at giving yourself the freedom to rest? Do you think you rest *too* much?
- ❧ How good do you think *I* am at giving *me* the chance to rest? Do you think I rest too much?
- ❧ Do you feel that I encourage you to rest, or do you think I am secretly annoyed when you take time out?
- ❧ How could I help you to get the type of rest you need?

A Suggested Prayer

Father, every day there is so much to accomplish. We confess that sometimes we make poor use of our time, but usually we are hard pressed to get it all done. As we have talked, we have discovered . . .

ROLES

Submit to one another out of reverence for Christ.
Ephesians 5:21

I t used to be so easy. When you got married, everyone knew who was responsible for what. No, it often
wasn't fair, and yes, it was often cruel. But it *was* clear.

The world is so different today. Each person's responsibilities seem to be up for grabs. Who does the shopping,
cleaning, cooking, dishes, diapers, discipline, finances?
And as soon as balance and clarity begin to emerge,
some change in the family seems to ruin the delicately
assembled understanding. It can be anything—a new job,
a child, a sense of restlessness or anxiety, an illness.

It is hard defining roles today. It takes pain, struggle,
and sacrifice in order to "submit to one another," but it's
all worth it. As each of us takes the time and energy to
listen, to care about the feelings of our friend and partner,
we strengthen the foundation upon which our marriage
is built.

"Out of reverence for Christ." If for no other reason,
we have a clear command from the Lord to swallow pre-
suppositions and hidden expectations and tangibly seek
to serve each other. It may not feel right, at least not at
first, but as we both focus on Jesus Christ in submitting
to one another, we will begin to see how rich and intimate
our marriage can be.

Society accepts no school, no book, no seminar as the final "right" answer on who does what in marriage. As a result of society's rejection of biblical standards, a man may feel this way:

Husband

I know some guys who go to work early, come home late, and expect to be treated like tired kings when they return. Another will stay home to be with the children and manage the household so his wife can pursue a career. As I fall somewhere in the middle, I am not at all sure if the things I do and don't do match my wife's needs, desires, and expectations. It would be easier for me if I could know what she thinks and be free to tell her what I need.

Because they have traditionally been expected to handle the household and children, it may be hard for some wives to find the right balance for both themselves and their marriage. Some women might express their feelings like this:

Wife

It is easy for me to feel taken advantage of and insignificant in my role as mother and homemaker. I love my children and enjoy being a mom, but it is often a thankless job that does not receive much recognition. Thus I am forced to examine where my true identity lies, and I ask myself, *What am I motivated by?* Do I really see these roles as important? Have I stopped to think how God sees my role?

LET ME ASK YOU THIS . . .

* What is your understanding of our individual roles in marriage? Are you happy with this understanding?

* Are there things we need to discuss and possibly change?
* Do you feel safe in talking to me about change in our tasks and marriage? Why, or why not?

A SUGGESTED PRAYER

Father God, You know how confusing it is for us to be married today. You know the many things that need to be done, and how tired we are. Give us the patience and the time to listen to each other, to tangibly love each other, so that we may learn how to move through the years united in spirit . . .

ROMANCE

Enjoy life with your wife, whom you love.

Ecclesiastes 9:9

♡

A long-time friend, who had been married twenty years, nearly exploded: "I feel like a kid again! I can't stop thinking about my wife, and I can't seem to hold it in. I'm sending her notes, having flowers delivered, and surprising her with fun, crazy dates that take weeks to plan. But I'll tell you this—I'm having a blast!"

Romance is God's idea—He invented it! We tend to think that anything fun, wild, or spontaneous is somewhat less than spiritual. What blasphemy—God wants us to be aggressive and extravagant in our love for each other.

Romance doesn't just happen, it is an ember that must be fueled and fanned in order to ignite. Romance can make the difference between an exciting marriage and one shackled with predictability and boredom.

To make the effort to plan the "perfect getaway," even for the evening, communicates volumes to your spouse about your love and commitment. Whatever form you choose—a short love note, a card sent in the mail, a walk at night, a surprise package with favorite "goodies," or breakfast in bed with a rose—romance can spark the fire in any marriage.

CONVERSATION STARTER

In many marriages, predictability is the norm and romance the exception, and some couples might feel like this:

Husband

There are many times through the day when I think about my wife, but I must admit that I don't tell her very often. I guess I figure that she knows I love her, but I rely on that a little too much. As I think about this, every excuse in the book comes to mind for why I don't do more, but they really aren't valid. I do love her, and I want to tell her and show her more often.

Wife

Romance is what keeps life in our marriage. It is the reason I can say that I am more in love with my husband today than I was years ago when we first met. But like anything, romance takes work and planning. Sometimes I find myself tempted to sacrifice a special getaway so that we can get some new item I've wanted. When I face a choice like that, I have to remember what I believe will be most important in the long run.

LET ME ASK YOU THIS . . .

- ❧ What is the most romantic thing I have ever done for you? What made it so special?
- ❧ List a few things that you consider romantic.
- ❧ When was our last romantic overnight outing? When would you like to do that type of thing again?

A SUGGESTED PRAYER

Father, thank You for the gift of romance. We confess to You and to each other that we often have allowed our circumstances, money, and schedules to become excuses for not enjoying each other. Help us to realize the joy we have when we find new ways to love each other . . .

SELF-ESTEEM

For you created my inmost being; you knit me together in my mother's womb. I praise you because I am fearfully and wonderfully made; your works are wonderful, I know that full well.

Psalm 139:13-14, A psalm of David

—————————————— ♡ ——————————————

E ven a casual glance at the world around us tells us how inadequate we are. Sitcoms reveal the "thirty-minute solution" to devastating family issues, the soaps let us see how beautiful *other* people look when they wake up, and the editors remove all the falls from the gymnastics meets. In our sterile environment, everybody is happy, healthy, beautiful, and smart.

It's no wonder so many people secretly struggle with identity and worth. A friend wrote, "I'm beginning to see myself as a small, insignificant cog in a massive, efficient machine. The things I fight for, strive to attain, and worry about are now appearing small and cheap. Who am I? Where do I fit?"

It is hard to fight the messages that permeate our lives. But the mirror of comparison—telling us how much we lack—is distorted, because no one is exempt. Even beauty queens lose sleep over their weight. The problem lies in the fact that we trust the reflection.

God's mirror tells a different story. When we look in the reflection of His Word, we see that He views us as "fearfully and wonderfully made."

You are created in His image, and He thinks you are wonderful, gifted, and worth loving. He proved it when

He died for you. As the old preacher said, "God don't make no junk, so get outta the junkyard!"

CONVERSATION STARTER
Poor self-esteem affects all of us, so men and women may express their feelings like this:

Husband
As I look around me, I sometimes wonder if I am the only one who feels insecure. Everyone else looks so confident, but I constantly compare and second guess myself. Then there are times when, for whatever reason, I look at others and thank the Lord I'm not like them! I guess the comparison game works both ways — we try to find those we have passed, and we hurt because of those we still chase.

Wife
I like myself pretty well. But there are those days when I occasionally catch myself thinking, "If only I were ten pounds thinner, or looked more like Sally, *then* I would feel better about myself." I guess I haven't really learned to love myself totally as I am. I wonder if I ever will.

LET ME ASK YOU THIS . . .
- How do the psalmist's words touch you? What does it mean to you that you are "fearfully and wonderfully made"?
- What are a few things you like about yourself?
- What are a few things you don't like about yourself?
- How can I help you realize more deeply how important you are to me and to God?

A SUGGESTED PRAYER
Father, forgive us for comparing ourselves to others — both those we look up to and those we disdain. Help us to be so convinced of Your love for us that we are free to love ourselves and others, just as we are . . .

SEX

Then Jacob said to Laban, "Give me my wife.
My time is completed, and I want to lie with her."
Genesis 29:21

Sexual intimacy *is* a fantastic and powerful gift in marriage. When exercised as an expression of the intimacy present in the relationship, it can be holy, free, and bonding. The marriage bed of an intimate friendship is filled with laughter and spontaneity. It is fun!

But the point of marriage is not sexual gratification.

Somehow, a long time ago, men initiated the notion that the act of sexual intercourse was a duty for their wives to fulfill. If intimacy and mutual interest were present, of course, it made sex only more pleasurable, but the bottom line was men's desire to be "satisfied." There are many reasons why this attitude has survived, but God never intended it. Sex is too precious, too sacred, to be forced or coerced.

Sex was never intended to be used as an instrument for selfish indulgence. We are all driven to seek intimacy, and for many of us, sex grants a temporary reprieve from that drive. It may lull us into thinking that we *are* involved intimately, and that this pleasure is all we need to bring us closer together. But the illusion is false, for sex without relational intimacy will divide, not unify.

Sexual games and power struggles abound in marriages. Most men desire greater frequency, while their wives are satisfied with less. What is the balance? Every couple must decide for themselves, as statistics and averages only cause us to compare, producing more guilt and frustration. But one thing is certain for sexual growth and unity. Every married couple must see as their primary priority the deepening of their love for and intimacy with one another. The more we talk, write notes, give gifts, and take time to be alone, or even simply get away together, our natural drive for sexual intimacy will flow freely.

CONVERSATION STARTER

In response to the topic of sexual interest, many men may state their feelings like this:

Husband

Before I was married I had a mental picture of having sex every day, with my wife always as interested in sex as I was. I had no idea how shallow my understanding of sexual relationships was, but I've sure learned! It took a while for the honeymoon to wear off, and as the years have progressed we have learned to listen to each other and to compromise. But sometimes when I watch a movie or find myself in a romantic mood, I revert back to my former expectations and get frustrated.

Sexuality is often viewed differently by women, as expressed here:

Wife

For me sex is an expression of my love for my husband. I have a very difficult time enjoying sexual intimacy unless I feel like we have caught up and connected on an emotional level first. After our hearts come together, then I long for intimacy. At this level, sex is the passionate expression of that closeness, and it is wonderful!

LET ME ASK YOU THIS . . .

- Why do you think God created sex?
- Prior to marriage, what were your expectations concerning sex?
- Are you satisfied with our present sexual understanding and situation? Is there anything we could do differently to enhance our sexual relationship?

A SUGGESTED PRAYER

Father, You know that we live in a sex-saturated society. We know that You must be grieved with the misuse of this gift You gave to us, and yet we believe that You are excited about sex in marriage. Help us to find the balance between an enjoyment of our sexual relationship and a godly understanding . . .

SOLITUDE

Very early in the morning, while it was still dark,
Jesus got up, left the house
and went off to a solitary place, where he prayed.
Mark 1:35

I f someone were to summarize the character of our culture in one word, it would be *busyness*. People never seem to find time for what's really important. Instead, urgent meetings, engagements, deadlines, and duties command their schedules. Everyone is running; everyone is frantically trying to stay ahead, or catch up.

Children are left alone, and so they follow their parents' model—soccer practice, piano lessons, ballet, Nintendo, MTV. They fall asleep with their headphones on, making sure there is no silence to disturb the blare. Their parents don't notice. After all, Jay Leno's hosting "The Tonight Show."

There was a day when people understood solitude. A child could play for hours in a field armed only with God's creation and her imagination. A man could go fishing and forget the worms. A couple could sit on the porch in the evening, enjoying the beauty of the stillness around them. Sadly, for most people, those days are gone.

Jesus knew the joy of solitude. And He knows it today. To be still, and know that God is there, is perhaps the deepest joy of faith. To sit quietly and hear the small, still voice of the Almighty brings meaning to the frantic pace of life. It reconstructs the soul.

It is often hard to find the time to be alone, and much harder to find a refuge where the gift of silence can be found. But it is possible, and God wants to meet you there.

CONVERSATION STARTER

In this hectic, crazy world, a man may think about solitude like this:

Husband

Some of my greatest memories are the times when I was all alone and quiet — in the mountains, by a stream, walking on the beach. I have never felt closer to God than when I have had the time to be by myself and think about Him and His love for me. I can't seem to capture that feeling very often, in fact it is a rare thing. But I *do* want to experience Him more often in this way.

A woman could have a different view of solitude, as expressed by this comment:

Wife

Quietness is so rare and hard to find in my world with three young children. And yet, it is a yearning of my heart to somehow learn to incorporate it into my life. I need to *make* time to be still, to ponder, to listen to the whispers of the Lord. I don't want to have to wait until this season of busyness passes, I need Him now!

LET ME ASK YOU THIS . . .

- ❧ How is Jesus' model of going off alone to pray an example to you?
- ❧ Have you ever tried to experience solitude with God? If so, what was it like? If not, why?
- ❧ Describe how you feel when you think of taking some time to be alone in a quiet place with God. If it is threatening, try to explain why.

🐝 What do you see as the top priorities for having a vital, growing relationship with Christ?

A SUGGESTED PRAYER

Father God, considering being somewhere alone with just You for any length of time is such a foreign idea. We would love the chance to slow down, to take long walks and breathe fresh air, but there never seems to be an opportunity. Help us to find solitude in the midst of our busyness, to slow down, to enjoy You . . .

A TYPICAL DAY

People were bringing little children to Jesus to have him touch them, but the disciples rebuked them.

Mark 10:13

♡

T he nerve of some people; actually believing that Jesus would have the time and the desire to hold little children! He is God with us, the Lion of Judah, the King of all kings, far too important for telling a bedtime story or wiping a tear.

The Bible is kind when describing our Lord's reaction as "indignant." If we imagine that God's interest is limited to doctrinal disputes, meditative prayer, and overseas missions, we reveal how little we understand His character. Jesus' identification with the everyday is what made Him so appealing to the masses, and it's what gives us hope for today.

Jesus lived in the mundane—walking miles at a time, eating with acquaintances, attending celebrations, touring with friends, speaking in a way that the most detached listener could understand. And, yes, especially touching, holding, loving little children. He appreciates life as the wild, tedious, and varied experience it is.

Regardless of the setting, Jesus both understands your labor and walks beside you in the midst of the daily battle. Do not look for Him only in the sacred, invite Him into the most ordinary of moments, and He will lift you to newfound heights.

Because the majority of life is lived in the valleys, and we tend to view a religious experience as extraordinary, many men may feel like this:

Husband

It is rare for me to experience Jesus Christ while getting ready for my day, or at the office, or while watching a ball game. Somehow it doesn't seem that He fits in the ordinary; I subconsciously feel that He deserves a nobler setting and mindset. It would change things for me, I think, if I did start looking for Him everywhere I go and in everything I do.

Many women find their days filled with the less-than-glamorous chores of daily life, and they may express their feelings this way:

Wife

Meals, carpools, cleaning, laundry, groceries . . . what about the "call" I received when I was younger to follow the Lord with my life? I considered the mission field; I wanted to make an impact for God's Kingdom. Is what I am *doing* of value to God? Going to work? Keeping house? Washing dishes? Is this all there is? I struggle with all that, but where did I get the idea that to be of value to God I needed to be doing measurable things, and seen by others as important? It is hard for me to remember that He is excited about me when I am on this treadmill of the ordinary.

LET ME ASK YOU THIS . . .

- ఴ Where do you most clearly experience God? On the mountain of the spectacular, or in the valley of the mundane?
- ఴ Do you think that most people find it hard to walk with Jesus in the ordinary? Explain.

ﻬ What is one tangible way that you can experience
   God more in the day-to-day routine? How can I
   help you?

A Suggested Prayer

Father, though our lives don't often reflect it, we want
desperately to recognize You in everything we do. Remind
us of Your presence, Lord. Grant us the wonder and
excitement of knowing You even in the midst of the
valleys . . .

AUTHORS

Chap Clark is the director of Youth Ministries at Denver Seminary, is an Associate Staff of Youth Specialties, and is on the Young Life staff in the Training Department. He has both a Master of Arts and a Master of Divinity degree from Fuller Seminary. A well-known speaker and writer in youth and family ministry, Chap has written several books, including *Next Time I Fall in Love*, a book for adolescents on healthy relationships.

Dee Clark, formerly on staff with Young Life, is involved in women's ministries, and partners with Chap as a conference facilitator on marriage, youth, and communication. She is an active candidate for a degree in counseling, and spends time ministering to high school girls in Young Life. The Clarks have been married for eleven years and have three children. They live in Denver, Colorado.